The Language *of* Justice

Interpreting for Legal Services

Training Manual

Isabel Framer; Marjory Bancroft, MA;
Lois Feuerle, JD, Ph.D; and Jean Bruggeman, Esq.

This training program was funded by a D.C. Council appropriation, created through the advocacy efforts of the D.C. Access to Justice Commission and the D.C. Consortium of Legal Services Providers and administered by the D.C. Bar Foundation. It was developed with the support and oversight of Ayuda.

The D.C. Bar Foundation provides underprivileged residents of the District of Columbia access to legal representation by funding legal services organizations and supports lawyers seeking to ensure that all residents have access to competent legal representation.

Ayuda, a community-based 501(c)(3) nonprofit organization founded in 1973, provides multi-lingual legal and social services for low income immigrants in DC, Maryland and Virginia.

The curriculum was developed by Cross Cultural Communications, an agency devoted to improving the access of Limited English Proficient residents to health care, education and community services.

Cross-Cultural Communications
10015 Old Columbia Road, Suite B-215
Columbia, MD 21046
Voice: 410-312-5599
Fax: 410-750-0332
ccc@cultureandlanguage.net
www.cultureandlanguage.net

6925 B Willow Street NW
Washington D.C. 20012
Phone (202) 387-4848
www.ayuda.com

Contents

The Authors

Ayuda and Cross-Cultural Communications would like to thank the writing team that made this project possible.

This curriculum represents the interface between the fields of legal and community interpreting. It was developed by four specialists from both of these fields, including an attorney who runs a project for legal interpreters.

On the legal interpreting side, the team was privileged to include two respected experts: Isabel Framer and Lois Feuerle. On the community interpreting side the team benefited from the expertise of Marjory Bancroft, while Jean Bruggeman provided valuable legal expertise both as an attorney and the director of a nonprofit legal interpreter bank.

Isabel Framer, a national consultant on language access, currently serves as Chair of the National Association of Judiciary Interpreters and Translators (NAJIT). She is a court-certified Spanish interpreter for over 15 years, a leading national advocate on language access and a national trainer who has provided expert witness testimony on legal interpreting across the county. She regularly trains legal interpreters, judges, law enforcement, attorneys and other court support services on interpreting and language access and has created many training curricula. As an interpreter, she has worked in a broad array of legal settings from federal courts and grand juries to nonprofit legal services, private attorney offices, law enforcement investigations and detention settings. A graduate of a medical interpreter training program, she has also performed community interpreting. She is the co-founder and former president of the Ohio Court and Community Interpreters Association. In addition to sitting on national and state boards as well as task forces, she presents regularly at conferences across the country and serves on the Supreme Court of Ohio's Advisory Committee on Interpreter Services.

Lois Feuerle, former Coordinator of Court Interpreter Certification, Testing and Training for the Oregon Judicial Department, holds a Ph.D. from the University of Kansas and a JD from the New York University School of Law. She is admitted to the New Jersey Bar. For five years she served as the Coordinator of Court Interpreting Services for the New York State Office of Court Administration; she was also the administrator for five years of the Translation and Interpreting Studies program at New York University. Her working languages are German and English. Certified by the American Translators Association (ATA) since 1991, she is on the list of approved translators for the International Monetary Fund. As one of the developers of the New Jersey German Court Interpreting Exam, Dr. Feuerle has been a grader of court interpreter certification tests for New Jersey, Wisconsin and Colorado and other Consortium states as needed. She has also served three terms as a member of the NAJIT Board of Directors and was recently elected to the ATA Board. She is the current Vice President of the Society for the Study of Translation and Interpreting. Dr. Feuerle is Chair of the ATA Honors and Awards Committee and has completed her second term on the Oregon Governor's Commission on Healthcare Interpreters, the body charged with establishing a certification process for medical interpreters in Oregon. She has extensive experience training interpreters and translators across the country.

Marjory Bancroft, Director of Cross-Cultural Communications, immigrated to the U.S. from French Canada and has lived in eight countries. She holds a BA and MA in French linguistics from Université Laval in Quebec and advanced language certificates from universities in Spain, Germany and Jordan. She has taught translation, French and English as a second language for two universities (in Canada and Jordan), for immigrant schools run by the Quebec Ministry of Immigration and for continuing education programs. She spent several years interpreting for health and human services and providing direct services to immigrants and refugees. She also directed a nonprofit community language bank of 200 interpreters and set up an immigrant health program. The co-author of the only nationally available 40-hour certificate program and train-the trainer's program for bilingual staff and community interpreters, she has developed nearly three dozen interpreter and cultural competence training curricula, including five train-the-trainer programs. Since 2001 she has directed Cross-Cultural Communications, a training and technical assistance agency devoted to interpreting and cultural competence in community services. Today she is a leading national advocate for professional interpreter training for bilingual employees and community interpreters. She speaks widely at conferences, served three years on the Board of the National Council on Interpreting in Health Care and currently serves on the National LEP Task Force run by the National Health Law Program.

Jean Bruggeman is an attorney admitted to the Maryland and District of Columbia bars and the Director of the Community Legal Interpreter Bank, a project of Ayuda in Washington D.C. Each year, Ayuda provides multilingual legal and social services to thousands of immigrants from over 80 countries. The Interpreter Bank is a nonprofit legal interpreter service intended to provide trained interpreters for civil legal services providers in the District of Columbia. The project offers specialized training for interpreters and service providers. It also tests participating interpreters for language proficiency. Prior to this project, she directed the Survivor Services Department for Boat People SOS, a national Vietnamese community-based organization, where she also led the Community Against Domestic Violence and Victims of Exploitation and Trafficking Assistance programs, supervised legal and social services staff, conducted outreach and education within the Vietnamese community and provided training and technical assistance to service providers around the country. She graduated from the Georgetown University Law Center and was awarded a Women's Law and Public Policy Fellowship to serve as the VAWA Attorney at Ayuda in Washington DC in 2000. Jean also holds an AB (Sociology/Anthropology) from Bryn Mawr College.

Collectively, the co-authors have authored dozens of publications. They belong to, or serve on, various membership organizations, nonprofit boards, coalitions, task forces and other organizations across the U.S. that support quality interpreting, legal services and equal access to public services.

The authors wish to thank the following individuals and organizations who served as the Community Legal Interpreter Bank's Advisory Board during the development of this curriculum. They provided vital input and support in the development of these materials: Professor Muneer I. Ahmad; Eric Angel, Esq.; Professor Susan Bennett; Rosa Carrillo; Marita Etcubañez, Esq.; Isabel Van Isschot; Karen Minatelli, Esq.; Lillian Perdomo; American University Washington College of Law; the Legal Aid Society of the District of Columbia; Multicultural Community Service; Asian Pacific American Legal Resource Center; La Clínica del Pueblo; and the D.C. Employment Justice Center.

Preface

The Language of Justice is a three-day program designed to train community and court interpreters who perform non-courtroom legal interpreting. Although this curriculum primarily addresses spoken interpreting, the ethical requirements and protocols discussed in this program will also benefit sign language interpreters. (Some of the skills involved and issues that may arise in legal interpreting will affect sign language and spoken interpreters differently.)

This program addresses legal interpreting performed outside the courtroom. *The Language of Justice* does not focus on in-court interpreted proceedings. Participants who have received 40 hours or more of professional interpreter training in any area (including conference, court, community/medical or general interpreting) are ideally suited to attend this program. *The Language of Justice* may also be presented to those who are new to the field of legal interpreting. The training manual for *The Language of Justice* is designed to help participants provide competent interpreting for legal services providers and can also serve as a training manual for interpreters who work in other non-courtroom legal or quasi-legal settings.

There are two core audiences for this manual: community interpreters and court interpreters. One goal of the curriculum is to ensure that community interpreters clearly grasp the differences between community and legal interpreting. Another objective is to help court interpreters work effectively in non-courtroom legal settings. The interpreters who graduate from this program should emerge with a clear understanding of the ethics, standards, requirements and role of the legal interpreter.

Currently, there is an urgent need for training programs for non-courtroom legal interpreters. Community interpreters, for example, often are expected to act as advocates or cultural brokers, and they may be tempted to do so even when they perform legal interpreting. Such activities may be acceptable in community interpreting, but they can be problematic and even prohibited in settings that involve attorneys, and/or paralegals, or in law enforcement and domestic violence settings, to name a few. All too often, community interpreters are sent out to perform legal or quasi-legal interpreting without any guidance on how legal interpreting differs from community interpreting. In many cases, they may even be unaware whether they are performing community or legal interpreting. Without clear guidance, an interpreter in legal settings may inadvertently have an adverse impact on the Deaf, Hard-of-Hearing or Limited English Proficient (LEP) individual's case and could undermine the attorney's effectiveness.

Conversely, few training materials for court interpreters discuss in depth how different legal interpreting is outside the courtroom, which is where most of a lawyer's work is performed. For example, most court settings are adversarial and require a public record, whereas most encounters outside the courtroom are collaborative and private: the attorney and legal team, work actively on the client's behalf to secure a just and beneficial outcome. Sometimes the rigid procedures and guidelines for court interpreting do not transfer well to other legal settings, such as attorney-client interviews. Interpreters need explicit guidance for such interviews since the legal outcome may depend on the quality and integrity of the interpreter's performance.

This curriculum is dedicated to supporting all legal interpreters and showing how they can uphold the highest standards of the legal interpreting profession in collaborative settings like attorney-client interviews. The project was created and funded by lawyers through the D.C. Bar Foundation and administered by Ayuda, a nonprofit agency that provides legal services. It has benefited at every stage of its development from the direct input of attorneys who work with limited English speakers and the Deaf and Hard of Hearing.

The authors wish to thank Ayuda and the D.C. Bar Foundation for the opportunity to collaborate on this groundbreaking project. We welcome feedback and hope that the program benefits legal interpreters everywhere. The goal of this project is to support quality interpreting and equal access to justice for the LEP community.

Isabel Framer
ISAINTERP@aol.com
330-665-5753

Lois Feuerle
LoisMarieFeuerle@cs.com
503-236-5593

Marjory Bancroft
mbancroft@cultureandlanguage.net
410-750-0365

Jean Bruggeman
jean@ayuda.com
202-387-4848

Program Goal *and* Objectives

GOAL
To train community and court interpreters to interpret for nonprofit legal services providers

UNIT I
Procedures and Ethics (7 hours)

Objective 1:   The interpreter will discuss the requirements for legal interpreters.

Objective 2:   The interpreter will exhibit a sound understanding of relevant codes of ethics.

Objective 3:   The interpreter will demonstrate the correct application of a code of ethics and standards of practice to ethical dilemmas and simulated encounters.

UNIT II
Linguistic Mediation (7 hours)

Objective 1:   The interpreter will demonstrate sound decision-making about when and how to provide linguistic mediation.

Objective 2:   The interpreter will model the steps for linguistic mediation.

Objective 3:   The interpreter will develop linguistic mediation techniques and strategies.

UNIT III
Interpreting for Legal Services (6 hours)

Objective 1:   The interpreter will demonstrate knowledge of the U.S. legal system.

Objective 2:   The interpreter will model how to handle requests from clients and attorneys.

Objective 3:   The interpreter will review the terminology required for non-courtroom legal interpreting.

Final Assessment (1 hour)

A written assessment will evaluate participants' knowledge of the curriculum.

Definitions

A number of technical terms are used in this training manual. They are defined below, with annotations. Definitions are by the authors unless otherwise noted.

Attorney-client privilege

Protection of confidential communications between a client and her attorney, invoked according to rules of evidence in response to a request, during a court case, for the disclosure of confidential information.

Certified court interpreter (legal interpreting)

Interpreters may be certified by several different official entities, *e.g.*, National Center for State Courts Consortium test, the Federal Court Interpreter Certification examination, or the NAJIT certification examination. Note that there is not a test available for every language. Note also that these certifications are not necessarily equivalent since certification criteria and structure of each of these tests is different. Moreover, some entities have continuing education requirements that must be met at periodic intervals in order to maintain certification.

Certified medical interpreter (or certified community interpreter)

A professional interpreter who is certified as competent by a professional organization or government entity through rigorous testing based on appropriate and consistent criteria. Interpreters who have had limited training or have taken a screening test administered by an employing health, interpreter or referral agency are not considered certified. *National Council on Interpreting in Health Care (www.ncihc.org)*

Chuchotage

A form of whispered simultaneous interpreting (see below) that does not require the use of special equipment as it is performed by the interpreter whispering directly to the listener(s).

Community interpreting

Interpreting that takes place within a community setting, typically for public and nonprofit services.

Confidentiality

Practice of treating information as private. Confidentiality is one of the key elements of the attorney-client relationship and of the interpreter's relationship with both the attorney and the attorney's client.

Consecutive mode

The conversion of a speaker or signer's message into another language after the speaker or signer pauses, in a specific social context. *Definition from ASTM International.*

Court interpreting

Interpreting in the courtroom or for an official legal proceeding. The interpretation is preserved on the record or transcript of the hearing, deposition or trial. Court interpreting is a subcategory of legal interpreting.

Interpreting

The rendition of an oral or signed message into another oral or signed language.

Legal interpreting

Interpreting related to legal processes and proceedings, including but not limited to lawyer-client representation, prosecutor-victim/witness interviews, and law enforcement communications.

Legal services

Assistance with a legal matter, including giving legal advice, filing documents, sending correspondence, and representation in official hearings and other legal proceedings.

Legal services providers

Individuals and organizations that provide legal services. The term is generally used to refer to a non-profit organization, but the term is not exclusive. For-profit providers are generally referred to as law firms.

Limited English Proficiency (LEP)

Individuals who do not speak English as their primary language and who have a limited ability to read, write, speak, or understand English can be "limited English proficient" or "LEP" These individuals may be entitled to language assistance with respect to a particular type of service, benefit, or encounter. (*U.S. Department of Justice, LEP Policy Guidance for DOJ Recipients*)

Linguistic mediation

Any act or utterance by the interpreter that briefly suspends the interpreted session or takes place outside it and is intended to remove a *linguistic* barrier to communication.

Mediation

A term used in community interpreting in the U.S. and around the world to refer to any act or utterance by the interpreter that briefly suspends the interpreted session or takes place outside it and is intended to remove *linguistic, cultural or systemic barriers to communication, service delivery and equal access to services.*

Remote interpreter

An interpreter not physically present at the interview site who interprets from a remote location by telephone or videoconferencing equipment.

Register (or "Language register")

Level of language. "High register" usually indicates formal, elevated or highly technical language, often with complex syntax. "Low register" may indicate language that is casual, colloquial or slang.

Sight translation

The oral rendition of a written document into another language.

Simultaneous mode

Interpreting that is performed more or less at the same time the original speaker is speaking, albeit with a brief time lag.

Source language

The language *from* which an interpreter renders an oral or signed message. The term source language likewise refers to the language from which a translator renders a written message into another language.

Target language

The language *into* which an interpreter renders an oral or signed message. The term target language likewise refers to the language into which a translator renders a written message.

Translation

The written rendition of a text in one language into a written text in another language.

Translator*

An individual who renders written texts in one language into written texts in another language.

Transparency

The act of ensuring that anything said or signed during an interpreted encounter is known by all parties to the encounter. In legal interpreting, it includes the additional requirement that everything said by the interpreter while performing linguistic mediation must be interpreted to both parties.

Unauthorized Practice of Law

Legal services that are not provided in accordance with the relevant Code of Professional Responsibility, or are provided by individuals who are not licensed to practice law in that jurisdiction, whether or not they have attended law school or are authorized to practice law in another jurisdiction.

Whisper (or whispered) interpreting

A form of simultaneous interpreting performed for a single individual or small group. Typically, it is performed during a public discourse in the source language. When it is performed with special equipment, at a distance from the individuals in need of interpreting, it is usually simply referred to as simultaneous interpreting (see above). When it is performed by an interpreter located in very close proximity to the individuals in need of interpreting, it may be referred to as *chuchotage* (see above).

---

* Interpretation and translation, while closely related, are not identical disciplines. Each area requires different knowledge, training and practice. Credentialing is different for each. Some practitioners are equally adept at both; others specialize in one discipline or the other. Although the public and media often use the terms interchangeably, in professional settings use *interpretation* or *interpreting* when referring to oral speech and *translation* when referring to written texts.

UNIT I

PROCEDURES AND ETHICS

Requirements *for* Interpreters *in* Legal Services

UNIT I, OBJECTIVE 1
Discuss the requirements for legal interpreters

Introduction

Legal interpreting is a vital profession. A qualified legal interpreter assists attorneys, courts, court support services and other justice partners to promote equal access to justice, support federal and state laws and helps to prevent grave miscarriages of justice by providing complete and accurate interpreting.

There is an urgent need for trained legal interpreters. The profession is expanding swiftly; a legal interpreter who speaks one of the nation's most needed languages may look forward to a rapidly developing career, particularly in urban areas. Certification for legal interpreters (discussed below) enhances these opportunities and promotes high standards in the field.

Legal interpreting refers to interpreting that is related to legal processes and proceedings, including but not limited to lawyer-client representation, prosecutor-victim/witness interviews, and law enforcement communications. Court interpreting is the most widely known sector of legal interpreting, but it constitutes only one segment of the field. For example, legal interpreting may also be needed for attorney-client interviews, in-custody interviews (*e.g.*, jail, prison, holding cells or juvenile detention), depositions, administrative hearings, mediation and arbitration.

This training program focuses primarily on interpreting within the attorney-client relationship, often referred to as "interview interpreting." Unit I offers an overview of the legal interpreting profession and compares court interpreting to non-courtroom legal interpreting. This unit also introduces the requirements and procedures that govern the conduct of legal interpreters. Finally, Unit I looks closely at codes of ethics and standards of practice that guide legal interpreters on how to apply the appropriate ethics and standards outside the courtroom.

Legal Interpreting

Description

The legal interpreting profession involves interpreting during legal processes and proceedings, including lawyer-client representation and in other justice settings. However, most books, articles and training manuals on the subject focus primarily, if not exclusively, on court interpreting.

A great deal of legal interpreting takes place outside the courtroom. This manual focuses on attorney-client interviews. The rules governing interpreting during attorney-client interviews also apply to many other non-courtroom settings, which may include:

- Immigration service interviews
- Arbitration
- Filing discrimination complaints (EEO complaints, Offices for Civil Rights, local Offices of Human Rights, etc.)
- School Board hearings
- Medical examinations for worker's compensation or Social Security Disability insurance (such exams may constitute medical and/or legal interpreting)
- Mediation, *e.g.*, between employers and employees, or for divorce and custody cases
- Interpreting for law enforcement
- Interpreting for the District Attorney's Office
- The sight translation of legal forms in any setting

These are only a few common examples from the field. Many other community services situations could entail, or result, in interpreting scenarios that have legal consequences. The guidance provided in this manual on how to interpret for legal services providers applies broadly to most sectors of non-courtroom legal interpreting.

Role of the Legal Interpreter

Inside or outside a courtroom, the role of the legal interpreter is to provide *complete, accurate and unbiased interpreting*. This requirement applies uniformly to attorney-client interviews, hearings or any other legal processes and proceedings.

In court, the interpreter typically restricts his or her role to interpreting except to request occasional linguistic clarifications. These requests may have some restrictions imposed by the court, the judge and the established procedures in court settings. However, attorney-client interviews and other non-courtroom legal settings often take place in a less formal, non-adversarial, and less structured environment. The formal and adversarial process in court (with its emphasis on an accurate record) may be counter-productive during a legal consultation. This program will explore in some depth what the legal interpreter is permitted to do outside the courtroom when there is a need to explore the complexity of linguistic communication.

The legal interpreter in an attorney-client interview is there to facilitate clear communication between the attorney and the client. This manual provides guidance on how to do so effectively while adhering to the ethical requirements and accepted standards of practice for the profession. However, at no time may the interpreter who works in legal settings outside a courtroom abandon the real task of the legal interpreter: *to provide complete, accurate and unbiased interpreting*.

An Overview of Legal Interpreting Skills and Procedures

A legal interpreter must, at a minimum, be able to:

1. Master the three interpreting modes: consecutive, simultaneous and sight translation.
2. Adhere to a code of ethics and customary standards of practice.
3. Perform a professional introduction.
4. Accurately render a message in first person.
5. Adopt effective positioning.
6. Take notes.
7. Enhance memory skills.
8. Conduct a pre-conference, where appropriate.
9. Perform linguistic mediation.
10. Master basic legal terminology.

Unit I offers guidance on how to adhere to a code of ethics and standards of practice and how to perform a professional introduction. It also addresses the question of positioning and offers role-play practice in first person.

Unit II reviews modes of interpreting and examines the most complex challenge for legal interpreters: linguistic mediation. Linguistic mediation can (and often does) take place outside the session, for example, it may occur during a pre-conference. How to conduct a pre-conference is also addressed in Unit II.

Unit III looks at legal terminology and the larger U.S. legal system, because legal terminology has no meaning without context.

Because this program lasts only three days, there will be no time to address note-taking or memory skills during the training. Some basic information on both subjects is addressed briefly in Unit II of this manual. However, the interpreter will have to continue his or her professional development beyond the training. The resource list that follows Unit III offers additional training opportunities as well as tools for practice and self-study and other helpful aids.

Background and History of Legal Interpreting

History

Because the United States is a nation of immigrants, legal interpreting has existed from the earliest times of recorded legal history in the U.S. Cases that involve interpreters date back to 1808, and state legislation mandating how legal interpreters should be appointed and paid was enacted in 1860 for New York, 1865 for Pennsylvania and 1884 for California. (González *et al*, 1991:5)

As a profession, however, legal interpreting, both within and outside the courtroom, was largely unregulated for well over a century. It was practiced by interpreters who had no formal training, no testing (of either source or target language or interpreting skills), no certification and no licensure. The uneven quality of legal interpreters was noted in courtrooms in a number of cases dating back to 1980 (Davis, 1980), and little attention was paid to legal interpreting outside the courtroom.

During the 1970s, the impact of increasing immigration was felt across the country. Unlike earlier waves of immigrants, who came largely from Europe, the new immigrants came from around the world. Today, according to the latest data from the U.S. Census Bureau, about half of our foreign-born residents come from Latin America and one quarter from Asia, while others come from Africa, Oceania, Europe and Canada. U.S. immigrants speak over 300 languages.

Language access and equal justice

The tension between preserving the integrity and affordability of a uniform justice system and accommodating the interests of a multitude of immigrants and native peoples with different traditions and languages predates the United States itself. For example, the Court Minutes for New Amsterdam contain numerous reports of parties appearing with or through their interpreter, required because the court at the time conducted business solely in Dutch. By the time the Dutch transferred what was to become New York City to England, some eighteen different languages were spoken there.

Over much of the twentieth century, however, the courts and other branches of government have been required to improve the ability of each person to stand equally before the court itself. Increasingly, particularly over the last half of the last century, attention has been paid to how issues such as poverty, capacity, language and other concerns outside the courthouse have impacted what is happening inside the courthouse.

One of the consequences of the civil rights movement was enactment of the Civil Rights Act of 1964, which more tightly wove a federal enforcement mechanism for equal treatment and access into the national legal and political fabric of our society. Included was Title VI, which provides that no person "shall, on the ground of race, color, or national origin, be excluded from participation in, be denied the benefits of, or be subjected to discrimination under any program or activity receiving Federal financial assistance."

Both before and since enactment of the Civil Rights Act, courts have repeatedly held that "national origin" is often defined by the characteristics associated with ancestry, and that one of those characteristics is language. In 2000, then-President Clinton signed Executive Order 13166, which recognized the substantial link between language and national origin, and imposed on entities that receive federal financial assistance and all parts of the federal Executive Branch an identical duty to develop and implement written plans, consistent with guidance issued by the Department of Justice, to address the needs of linguistic minority groups in the United States. In 1975, the U.S. Department of Justice amended its Title VI Coordination Regulations to require recipients of federal financial assistance to ensure that critical documents are translated into appropriate languages other than English when the assisted entity served significant numbers of an identifiable LEP group.

Recognizing these problems and their impact on the integrity of the federal judicial system, Congress passed the federal Court Interpreters Act in 1978 requiring (among other things) a process to certify interpreters, and the use of certified interpreters to address the language assistance needs of litigants. While directly applicable only to the federal judicial system, the Court Interpreters Act fueled new efforts to increase the use of certified or qualified interpreters in courts at the state and municipal level. Also in 1978, the National Association of Judiciary Interpreters and Translators (NAJIT) was founded. Today, NAJIT, which counts approximately 1,300 formal members, conducts conferences, training and testing programs; publishes a quarterly journal called Proteus; has developed a national Code of Ethics and Professional Responsibility for interpreters; and administers its own certification test in Spanish for court interpreters.

Passage of the Court Interpreters Act and Title VI, however, did not ensure that appropriately qualified interpreters were, as a practical matter, provided when and where they were needed. Moreover, despite a growing awareness in the 1990's as to the need for qualified interpreters in legal settings, the mechanism for developing and qualifying legal interpreters was neither fully understood nor adequately funded. The myth relied upon by many, was that the courts could appropriately rely upon the services of anyone who spoke two or more languages. In some cases, even these efforts at linguistic justice were limited to particular days or times during the week, when part-time language assistance providers were available. The legal and personal consequences of this myth and the policies it spawned have been tragic to both the integrity of the judicial process and the lives of LEP litigants, defendants and victims of crime.

The accelerating initiatives, loosely referred to as the "language access" movement, intended and designed to effectively address the needs of LEP communities at the state, local and federal levels have placed increasingly difficult demands on the legal and community interpreting professions. Those demands, in turn, have required language assistance providers to create or enhance programs to better train, certify and allocate the country's language resources.

Training programs

As a result of case law, statutes, court rules and Title VI language access requirements and policies, as well as the work of many who support access to justice through quality legal interpreting, a growing number of states have established certification and training programs for court interpreters. However, few such programs address legal interpreting in non-courtroom settings. In part, this may be because a number of statutes, case law, policies or ethical standards focus mainly on in-court interpreting while few policies and case law address non-courtroom legal interpreting.

Yet legal interpreters work in many settings outside the courtroom. These settings may include, but are not limited to, meetings with attorneys or paralegals in law firms or nonprofit agencies. They may also involve meetings with non-legal staff, such as advocates or caseworkers. The interpreter may also interpret for legal staff members that have no training on how to work effectively with interpreters.

In addition, outside the courtroom, and sometimes even within it, legal interpreting is often performed by interpreters who are not trained, tested or qualified to interpret. Certification for legal interpreters has been developed for many languages and is currently available in many of the 40 states that are members of the NCSC Consortium. Where certification does exist, many courts have been unable to obtain funding to train and test interpreters in languages other than Spanish. Some untrained/unqualified legal interpreters are bilingual employees who have neither been trained to interpret nor tested either for language proficiency or interpreting skills, and it is often unclear whether they are truly bilingual. Other unqualified interpreters who work in legal settings may include volunteers, advocates from faith-based and community-based organizations, family and friends and even children.

It is dangerous to use untrained and untested interpreters. The settings we address are connected with a legal process and can and will have an impact on the outcomes in-court or other legal proceedings. It is inappropriate, and potentially unethical, for lawyers and other legal services providers to use friends, family and children. Yet so far little has changed in the practice of using untrained interpreters in non-courtroom legal settings, in great part due to the lack of knowledge and training for legal staff, but also due to the limited financial resources available to many legal services providers. Moreover, there is a shortage of certified and qualified interpreters. Legal interpreting requires a unique set of professional skills, but little funding or training is available to teach interpreters these skills, especially those who speak languages other than Spanish.

Legal Interpreting and Other Interpreting Professions

Legal interpreting is an established profession. Many individuals may be under the impression that legal interpreting is subcategory of community interpreting, but this is not accurate. Although many community interpreters do interpret in legal settings, legal interpreting has its own ethics, standards and requirements and is governed by statute, court rules and/or case law, and these differ in many respects from the ethics, standards and requirements applicable to community interpreting. The two professions should not be confused.

One of the difficulties in trying to differentiate between different areas is that certain interpreting fields have become professionalized and are regulated by ethics and standards, while other areas are still only *sectors* of interpreting. Furthermore, the lines drawn between the sectors are not always clear. For example, it is fair to say that the only established interpreting professions in the U.S. are **conference** interpreting (trained conference interpreters often work in government and diplomatic arenas as well as the private sector); **legal** interpreting (where most employment opportunities are for court interpreters); and **medical** interpreting (currently the most professionalized sector of community interpreting).

Other areas of interpreting such as military, escort, media, business and general interpreting have as yet no established codes of ethics, standards of practice or official requirements. To remedy this problem, the American Translators Association has begun to explore the possibility of setting up a generalist certification program for interpreters that would be similar to its well-known certification program for translators.

While medical interpreting in the U.S. has its own national ethics and standards of practice (available at the website of the National Council on Interpreting in Health Care at **www.ncihc.org**), and the field is working hard to establish national medical interpreter certification, most experts agree that medical interpreting is only one subcategory of the larger profession of community interpreting.

*For purposes of this curriculum, participants should consider legal interpreting as an **autonomous** profession,* whether it is practiced inside or outside a courtroom. Any interpreter who performs legal interpreting should comply with the applicable local ethical requirements for court interpreters within that jurisdiction and with the NAJIT Code for judiciary interpreters and should not be guided by the ethical requirements for community, general or conference interpreters.

Legal Interpreting and Sign Language

Sign language interpreting for the Deaf and Hard of Hearing is a formal profession with national certification for interpreters. American Sign Language (ASL) is a language used by many Deaf and Hard of Hearing people in the U.S., although others speak Signed English, and/or other languages such as Mexican, German or French Sign Language.

As a profession, sign language interpreting supports high standards in the field, and a number of universities offer four-year degree programs for ASL interpreters. (Few such programs exist in spoken interpreting.) In addition, the Registry of Interpreters for the Deaf (RID), which administers the national certification program for sign language interpreters, awards the Specialist Certificate: Legal (SC:L) to interpreters "who meet specific criteria regarding prior certification, education and experience."

RID also has issued clear guidance about legal interpreting for sign language interpreters who perform legal interpreting. Sign language interpreters will find guidance on legal interpreting in the RID Standard Practice Paper on "Interpreting in Legal Settings" (**www.rid.org**). This paper makes clear that much of the legal interpreter's work takes place outside the courtroom, citing the examples of attorney-client conferences, investigations by law enforcement, witness interviews, real estate settlements, court-ordered treatment and education programs and administrative hearings. The paper also makes clear that sign language interpreters are governed by a different set of legal rules when interpreting for law enforcement than when interpreting for attorney-client interviews, while at the same time emphasizing that the interpreter is at all times governed by RID ethical standards.

The paper then explores in general, what the term "qualified legal interpreter," means for sign language interpreters, including standard practices, staffing for legal interpreting appointments, potential risks, the importance of preparing for assignments, ethical concerns and standard practices in court interpreting.

Those interpreters who pursue the SC:L will gain a broader perspective and deeper understanding of the ethical requirements, best practices and acceptable standards for legal interpreting. While *The Language of Justice* curriculum focuses primarily on spoken interpreting, much of the information presented here will also serve to deepen the sign language interpreter's understanding of legal interpreting, its requirements and challenges, the "culture" of interpreting for legal services, and the particular concerns about interpreting for attorney-client interviews.

Court Interpreting

Description

Court interpreting is an important sector of legal interpreting. Because legal interpreting has evolved largely out of court interpreting, it is important for legal interpreters to have a sound understanding of court interpreting in order to see how some of its culture and requirements may differ, however slightly, from some of the requirements for interpreting in non-courtroom legal settings.

The courtroom is a crucible. Peoples' lives and fates hang in the balance. A legal case becomes a public proceeding in which the court acts to determine the competing interests of the parties. It is perhaps the drama of the courtroom, the adversarial and public nature of the proceedings, the high stakes involved in both criminal and civil cases, and the formal record that is made for later review that have made court interpreting the focus of (and often a proxy for) the profession of legal interpreting as a whole.

The court interpreter is an officer of the court whose primary purpose is to assist all of the parties in the administration of justice by providing complete, accurate and unbiased interpreting. Interpreters who work in a judicial setting may interpret for federal, state or municipal courts. Their work might involve complex cases lasting several weeks or proceedings as short as only a few minutes. Court interpreters may be requested for either criminal or civil cases.

Today, court interpreting has strict protocols, procedures, ethics and standards. Many judges, attorneys, law enforcement and other court officials receive training on the role of court interpreters.

Most state courts screen and assess their court interpreters and/or certify them. Despite these improvements, there is still a lack of knowledge within the legal profession about the training, testing and certification requirements for court interpreters. The U.S. continues to experience a shortage of qualified court interpreters throughout the justice system. As a result, due process, equal protection and access to justice remain elusive for millions of Deaf and LEP residents.

In most cases, their work takes place in a highly structured and often rigid environment where the interpreter is expected to do little more than interpret, and yet the parties present fail to understand the complexities of language, culture or interpreting.

—*Mikkelson (1998)*

Background

Court interpreting has its own unique history. Whereas other types of interpreting have evolved largely in response to the needs of their clients, court interpreting has been shaped by the Consortium Model Code of Professional Conduct for Court Interpreters, case law, statutes and rules internal to the court system.

All legal settings are governed by statute, court rule and case law that interpreters must adhere to. This is one reason why the ethics requirements for legal interpreters are strict, just as they are for lawyers or for anyone else working within the justice system.

Over the years—thanks to the efforts of court interpreters, NAJIT and other interpreter and translator associations, administrative offices of state courts, National Center for State Courts, judges and lawyers, advocates and others—the field of court interpreting has emerged as the most professionalized sector of legal interpreting.

The administrative and cultural features of the courtroom have heavily influenced Court interpreting. This may be one of the reasons that court and community interpreters often feel they are looking at each other across a great divide. They inhabit two different worlds. They comport themselves differently (for example, interpreters in the courtroom dress and behave more formally than most community interpreters). They draw different boundaries. Even outside a courtroom, court interpreters tend to maintain strict boundaries. Community interpreters often find themselves developing somewhat personal relationships with clients. When a fatal diagnosis is announced, when a parent learns a child will be expelled or when someone loses their benefits, some community interpreters might hold the client's hand or otherwise try to comfort them. Court interpreters must refrain from such personal behavior.

[In 1979] Dr. Benmaman agreed to help out in a court hearing where "some Spanish would be spoken." It was the first time she set foot in the United States District Court in Charleston. She found fifteen Colombian and Panamanian defendants, ringed by fifteen attorneys and court personnel. A vessel laden with marijuana had been seized; the defendants, crew members, spoke Spanish only. Everyone was at a loss. One interpreter for 15 defendants, a courtroom where no one was familiar with the notion of an interpreter, let alone her role, and no one knew how to go about informing non-English speakers of their rights.

—Ieraci (2004)

The Work of the Court Interpreter

The work of the court interpreter is to assist in the administration of justice and to ensure the creation of an accurate court record through complete, accurate and unbiased interpreting. Everything that the court interpreter does should further the goals of ensuring the integrity of the judicial process and an accurate court record. In the criminal context, there is the added task of enabling a defendant to be truly "present" at his or her own trial, thereby ensuring the defendant's constitutional right to confront his or her accusers.

Among legal professionals, however, some confusion continues to exist as to the purpose and role of the court interpreter. Is the interpreter on hand primarily to support an accurate court record? Or is the interpreter's real purpose to help the Deaf or LEP party understand what is taking place? Or are both goals equally important? When is the court interpreter expected to assist parties to the process? Should the interpreter interpret only when Deaf or LEP witnesses testify, or should the interpreter provide a simultaneous interpretation for the Deaf or LEP party of all that transpires in court?

In civil proceedings, the confusion may be even greater because there are fewer constitutional protections than in criminal proceedings. Some states have taken measures to clarify this confusion; they clearly describe the role and practice of the court interpreter in civil matters and ensure the presence of an interpreter. In other states, the confusion persists.

To clarify some of these ambiguities, we must keep in mind that court interpreters are summoned to assist in the administration of justice. The court must understand and be understood, defendants and litigants must be present and understand the nature of the charges and/or proceedings, defendants or litigants need to be able to consult with their attorneys and to hear accurate testimony in order to competently participate in their own defense and proceedings, and the court must ensure that there is an accurate record for subsequent review if necessary. Consequently, the interpreter's role is to assist all of the parties by providing accurate, complete and unbiased interpretation. The interpreter, like the court reporter or judge is a neutral officer of the court with her primary obligation to the judicial process and not the individual.

Court Interpreter Certification

Question: Why should a legal interpreter be concerned about court certification if he or she does not plan to interpret in court?

Answer: Certification for court interpreters provides the highest credential available for legal interpreters who wish to demonstrate their professionalism, knowledge of specialized terminology, skills, commitment and mastery of legal interpreting.

A court interpreter **certification** test should assess the interpreter's *skills* in legal interpreting, that is, the ability to perform in the three modes of interpreting required by statute in English and the other language (simultaneous, consecutive and sight translation) and should also include legal and other specialized terminology in both the source and target language as well as interpreter ethics. Some, but not all, courts may include a translation component as part of the certification process. A language proficiency test assesses only the interpreter's *language ability* to determine whether the interpreter is truly bilingual; it does not assess interpreting skills.

A **language proficiency** test is typically used to determine the interpreter's readiness to take a court certification examination or as a screening for legal interpreters who speak languages for which no certification test has been developed.

To pass the court interpreting certification exam, the candidate must possess almost native-like fluency in both the source and target language.

State Certification

In 1995, the National Center for State Courts (NCSC) established the Consortium for State Court Interpreter Certification ("the Consortium"). The Consortium provides state courts with a certification process in legal interpreting that is well established and meets the criteria requirements for a valid and reliable testing instrument. NCSC created this multi-state partnership in part to develop court interpreter certification tests for member states, achieve economies of scale and create standards for identifying proficient, qualified court interpreters.

Individual states develop their own certification programs, which vary slightly from state to state. States may choose to opt out of or to use the written portion of the Consortium exam as a language proficiency screening test for both the certified and the non-certified languages, while other states may require a separate language proficiency test. The written portion of the exam includes general English vocabulary, grammar, usage, idioms, legal terminology and questions on ethics and professional conduct. Some states require that the written portion be passed before the candidate is permitted to take the oral test; other states do not require the written test. The oral test is designed to assess the three modes of interpreting required by statute: simultaneous, consecutive and sight translation. Interpreters who fail the oral or written portion of the certification exam may re-take the test again, and many do.

States have varying provisions in place for re-taking the exam. After passing both written and oral tests, attending the two-day orientation, passing an ethics test, undergoing a criminal history check and fulfilling additional requirements, the candidate is sworn in and receives state certification with an identification number. *In some cases a picture ID that includes the certification number is issued.*

The Consortium tests are currently available in at least 18 languages: Arabic (modern standard; Egyptian colloquial; and Levantine colloquial), Bosnian/Croatian/Serbian, Cantonese, French, Haitian Creole, Hmong, Ilocano, Korean, Laotian, Mandarin, Portuguese, Russian, Somali, Spanish, Turkish and Vietnamese. Abbreviated tests are available in Italian and German. (Note that not all tests are available in the three modes of interpretation: simultaneous, consecutive and sight translation.) Tests for other languages, such as Marshallese, Chukkese, Hindi and Panjabi (Eastern) are under development.

There are two types of test. The standard model includes testing in simultaneous, consecutive and sight translation modes (in both directions). The "abbreviated" model may include sight translation and simultaneous interpreting or only simultaneous interpreting and language proficiency in both English and/or the other language. See **www.ncsconline.org** for details. The Consortium tests are designed to ensure that interpreters are qualified to interpret in legal settings, thereby promoting equal protection, due process and access to justice for LEP individuals. Without qualified interpreters, the courts cannot function efficiently and effectively, and the integrity of the judicial process can be put at jeopardy. Many of the 40 member states have already implemented certification and qualification requirements as well as court rules and a Code of Professional Responsibility (code of conduct) for court interpreters. The remaining member states have begun the process. In addition, some states such as California and New York, created their own certification programs prior to the founding of the Consortium.

The Consortium certification exam was developed according to rigorous standards, and the Consortium has established strict protocols for its administration. Except for California and New York, which have their own validated certification programs for court interpreters, and the federal court interpreter certification exam, (discussed below) the Consortium test is the only spoken language interpreter credential accepted in state courts, with the exception of those state courts that accept NAJIT certification. Some states but not all, have reciprocal agreements whereby an interpreter certified by one Consortium member state can be certified in another state without re-taking the Consortium exam.

NAJIT Certification

As a national professional association for judiciary interpreters, NAJIT created a certification test to accredit its members and uphold high standards for the profession. The test was created by NAJIT's certification arm, the Society for the Study of Translation and Interpretation, Inc. (SSTI). It was, and remains, the only national exam for interpreters and translators developed, implemented and administered by and for legal interpreters and translators. The NAJIT exam includes both a written and oral component, in addition to an extensive legal translation component, and seeks to create a uniform standard for interpreters and translators working in legal settings throughout the U.S. Currently it is offered in Spanish.

In 2006, the NAJIT Board of Directors created a Certification Commission, which acts as the governing body for the NJITC certification process. Translators and interpreters who hold NAJIT certification must meet a Continuing Education requirement in order to maintain their certification. For more information, go to **www.najit.org**.

Federal Certification

Federal court interpreters are required by statute to be certified (see 28 USC Section 1827). However, the statute contains a provision stating that, if no certified interpreter is reasonably available, the court may use the services of an "otherwise qualified" interpreter. The federal certification test, also administered by NCSC, is generally similar to the Consortium test for state court interpreters.

The federal court interpreter certification exam is currently offered every other year, and is currently available only in Spanish, although in the past it was also offered in Navajo and Haitian Creole. See **www. ncsconline.org** for details.

Steps to Certification

Consortium members provide a mandatory basic orientation for all interpreters who will work for the court system (see below). Some states may have additional requirements, such as a written test of language proficiency, a written ethics test, a translation component and/or a criminal records check. Only upon passing the certification test and completion of the individual state's requirements, will interpreters be certified. For details regarding each state's requirements, see **www.ncsconline.org**.

Court Interpreter Orientation

In most Consortium member states, an orientation to court interpreting is given to prospective court interpreters. This orientation, which typically lasts two days, is offered to interpreters of any language. It introduces them to the fundamental work of the court interpreter, including interpreter ethics and legal terminology.

Court Interpreter Training

Language-specific skills training in legal interpreting is often difficult to find. Where such programs exist, most are typically available only in Spanish. Due to funding constraints and a lack of qualified trainers, many interpreters find that no training is available in their state.

If a state court does not offer skills-based training, interpreters must look for training offered by other entities in other states. The cost of travel and tuition makes such training expensive, particularly if interpreters are not able to make sufficient income to justify such expenses.

Quality training is available, however. Interpreters may attend workshops at conferences hosted by interpreter associations such as the National Association of Judiciary Interpreters and Translators (NAJIT) or by the American Translators Association (ATA). Some state court interpreter services programs and/or local interpreter associations also provide quality training. Interpreters can also attend community college or university-based interpreting programs such as those offered by the University of Arizona and MA programs such as those offered by the Monterey Institute of International Studies in Monterey, California, or the University of Charleston, South Carolina.

Court Interpreter Registries

Interpreters in NCSC Consortium member states who attend an orientation workshop and fulfill other requirements are often listed in a court interpreter registry for the state. Those who are certified are clearly noted on the list. However, when no certified interpreter is available for the particular language needed, an interpreter on the list who is registered but not certified may be called in to interpret. Unfortunately, many 'registered' interpreters have not received any training in interpreter skills and ethics and have not been subjected to any language proficiency or interpreter skills testing. Therefore, their qualifications and skills can vary greatly.

Legal Interpreting and Court Interpreting

Court interpreting is a well-established profession in the U.S. due to court rules, statutes and case law as well as the work of professional organizations. Court interpreting is also well established in other countries, including many European nations, Canada and Australia (see **www.cttic.org** and **ausit.org**) as well as parts of Latin America and South Africa (Moeketsi, 2003).

However, legal interpreting outside of the courtroom has been less formally established and is slightly different than interpreting in court. While the interpreter's *role* remains the same in both settings (to provide complete, accurate and unbiased interpreting), the interpreter's conduct will change somewhat in less formal non-courtroom settings.

That said many aspects of legal interpreting apply both inside and outside the courtroom. Legal interpreters in all settings must always:

- Interpret accurately and completely
- Adhere to a code of ethics
- Adopt professional conduct
- Follow accepted standards
- Inform the parties of real or perceived potential conflicts of interest
- Represent credentials accurately
- Request clarification of terms or utterances they do not understand
- Clarify linguistic ambiguity, where necessary and permitted

However, certain differences between the functions performed by legal interpreters inside and outside a courtroom should be noted (see Chart 1).

In court, the interpreter must conduct herself as a neutral, impartial officer of the court whose loyalty is owed solely to the integrity of the judicial process. This impartiality should also be maintained in the attorney-client setting. However, in the culture of attorney-client relationships, interviewing and counseling create a less rigid, more compassionate environment than most court settings.

The process of non-courtroom legal interpreting is therefore somewhat more flexible, less formal and less constrained than in the courtroom. Some of the time urgency and many of the procedural issues surrounding court interpreting may be absent in these meetings. The attorney's objective is to promote the identification and the fulfillment of the client's goals.

In order to avoid critical misunderstandings, an attorney, paralegal or other support staff person may want to encourage a sense of openness and exploration during meetings with the client and may want the interpreter to help the attorney do so. In an attorney's office, there is not the same sense of finality that a courtroom demands. However, in either case, the ethical requirements must be followed.

Finally, when comparing court interpreting to attorney-client interviews, it should be noted that the attorney's role is to be the client's advocate. Advocacy is the lawyer's responsibility, not the interpreter's. The interpreter is not permitted to act as an advocate.

CHART 1:
Court Interpreting and Non-Courtroom Legal Interpreting

1. The courtroom is an adversarial setting for the parties, in which the interpreter must maintain neutrality. In contrast, legal interpreting in other settings, such as attorney-client interviews, is typically collaborative.

For example, in attorney-client interviews, the client, attorney and interpreter work on the "same side." They seek a shared understanding.

2. In court, the interpreter works for the court. In non-courtroom settings, the legal interpreter typically works for the attorney providing the legal service.

For example, in a courtroom the interpreter answers to a judge and must follow the judge's directions on procedure. In a meeting with an attorney, the interpreter must work within the context of the attorney-client relationship and follow the guidance of the attorney.

3. Court interpreting requires that the interpreter comply with the rules of the court. Legal interpreting outside the courtroom may include other constraints.

For example, in attorney-client interviews, the interpreter must respect the attorney's code of ethics. A lawyer could be held liable for the interpreter's misconduct.

4. A central purpose of the court interpreter's work is to help the court administration to function smoothly and to ensure an accurate record for subsequent review. In attorney-client interviews, a central purpose is to facilitate communication between the attorney and the client.

In a lawyer's office, the objective is to establish a relationship of trust and mutual understanding in order to facilitate an exchange of information and ideas and to build a case that advances the client's interests.

Cultural and Linguistic Barriers

Court interpreting typically prohibits the interpreter from interrupting except to request or provide clarification. Even if the court interpreter senses deep cultural barriers or confusion, the interpreter must remain silent. This restriction can be emotionally difficult for court interpreters, who often wish to give information or guidance that might help those present to understand each other better.

Court interpreters are normally required to interpret the source material "without editing, summarizing, deleting, or adding while conserving the language level, style, tone, and intent of the speaker" (Gonzáles et al. 1991: 16) even though a verbatim interpretation that preserves meaning "is literally impossible" (1991: 17). As a result, today the trained legal interpreter is taught that literal or verbatim interpreting is not what is sought but rather the closest natural equivalent. When judges and attorneys occasionally request the interpreter to interpret "verbatim," they really mean that the interpreter should interpret accurately.

Examples of Cultural Barriers

[In parts of South Africa, certain individuals in court may] tend to use a lot of gesticulation in their speech. For instance, to the prosecutor's question: "How many children do you have?" the witness's answer was: "My children are these many (with his thumb up to indicate the number six)." [...] Colour is often explained by pointing at anything similar in the courtroom. Size, length and distance are also explained in terms of what is observable; for instance, a person is as tall as that policeman at the door, or slightly shorter than that man next to the window. The use of African ideophones in the expression of sound or intensity by using mainly onomatopoeic words, is not known in English or Afrikaans. The linguistic phenomenon of polysemy is also rife. The Nguni verb stem -bamba normally means "to hold", but its meaning may shift with the context to mean sexual assault; robbery; arrest; withhold; or to take a route.

—Moeketsi (2003)

For example, in Spanish "*Sentí que tocaran la puerta*," means literally, "I felt the door knock." But that rendering is inaccurate. To interpret the statement accurately, the interpreter would have to say, "I heard a knock at the door." Yet even accuracy and completeness of interpretation will not always promote mutual understanding. Perhaps the single greatest challenge that faces the legal interpreter outside the courtroom is *how to handle a barrier to communication*. This curriculum provides specific guidance on cultural and linguistic barriers to communication in Unit II.

Community Interpreting
Description

Community interpreting involves any interpreting that takes place within the community. Two primary purposes of community interpreters are:

- To promote equal access to public services.

- To facilitate communication between members of the community who do not share a common language.

Most professional community interpreting takes place in government or nonprofit services, in three primary sectors:

- Health care

- Education

- Human and social services

Background and History

Community interpreting is a vital and vibrant profession. Community interpreters work in hospitals, schools, human services and other sectors such as housing, transportation and crisis intervention. They may save lives, promote public health and avert tragedies while supporting equal access to public and community services.

However, the profession has not yet matured. Despite federal, state and local laws that mandate the use of interpreters in public services, most community interpreting is still not performed by trained and qualified professionals. Instead, family and friends, untrained bilingual staff and other ad hoc interpreters are often relied upon to interpret, whether or not they are truly bilingual.

Qualified Interpreters Are:

- Professionally trained
- Tested for language proficiency
- Tested for interpreting skills

Legal and Community Interpreting

There are similarities between the professions of community and legal interpreting. Professional community interpreters, like legal interpreters, must adhere to a code of ethics. Like legal interpreters, they must also:

- Follow accepted standards of practice.

- Interpret accurately and completely.

- Adopt professional and appropriate conduct.

But there are some critical differences. Community interpreting is still an emerging profession. It may permit or require behaviors that legal interpreters are not permitted to perform, for example:

- Maintain trust among all parties.

- Facilitate communication across cultural differences by alerting all parties present to significant cultural misunderstandings.

- Advocate for working conditions that support quality interpreting.

- Engage in advocacy.

Healthcare interpreting, also known as medical interpreting, is the most professionalized sector of community interpreting. A national code of ethics and national standards of practice were published by the National Council on Interpreting in Health Care in 2004 and 2005 respectively (available at **www.ncihc.org**). These ethics and standards are often applied in other areas of community interpreting, such as human services and educational interpreting.

—NCIHC (2005)

When May a Community Interpreter Engage in Advocacy?

Even for community interpreters, advocacy should be engaged in rarely. (Legal interpreters are generally prohibited from engaging in advocacy.) In general, if the client's health, well being or dignity is at risk, and/or equal access to a public service is in jeopardy, the community interpreter may *"speak out to protect an individual from serious harm, or advocate on behalf of a party or group to correct mistreatment or abuse."* (NCIHC 2004)

Roles of the Community Interpreter

In spoken interpreting, the community interpreter is often considered to have four roles (Roat 1999). They are:

- **Conduit** (interpret accurately and completely)
- **Clarifier** (intervene to clear up linguistic misunderstandings)
- **Culture broker** (intervene to overcome cultural misunderstandings)
- **Advocate** (intervene to address a situation of danger, mistreatment or abuse)

In addition, many community interpreters are expected to *check for understanding, provide client support and help fill out forms*. Indeed, interpreters perform a great deal of work for LEP clients and providers *outside* the interpreted encounter. While the appropriateness of having an interpreter perform such work is a disputed topic within the profession, it is still common for community interpreters to perform various tasks for clients, particularly interpreters who are also bilingual staff. Often they work with LEP clients before and/or after

the interpreted encounter. Though the profession may disapprove of some of these practices, many community interpreters are still called upon to:

- Perform basic intake.
- Make phone calls to LEP clients to pass on information.
- Make phone calls to other agencies at the LEP client's request.
- Perform sight translation in the absence of a service provider.
- Accompany the client to other appointments.
- Give directions.
- Repeat instructions from the provider.
- Sight translate personal correspondence and bills for the client.
- Answer the client's questions before or after a session.

Developed by author Cynthia Roat and the Cross-Cultural Health Care Program in Seattle, the model of incremental intervention for medical—not legal—interpreters (a model often displayed as a pyramid) suggests that the healthcare interpreter should restrict her work primarily to the "conduit" role, *i.e.*, interpreting. The other three interpreter roles of *clarifier*, *culture broker* and *advocate* should be engaged in progressively less often, with advocacy being the role most rarely adopted. The rationale behind this model is that the three non-conduit roles progressively distance the interpreter from the basic task and also entail more risk.

—Roat (1999)

Requirements for Interpreters in Legal Services

Broadly speaking, the interpreter who sets out to interpret for legal services providers should know three things:

    a. What the interpreter *must* do and *may not* do.

    b. How to execute an assignment.

    c. How to interpret effectively.

This section provides a general overview of the requirements and procedures for legal interpreting (see Chart 2).

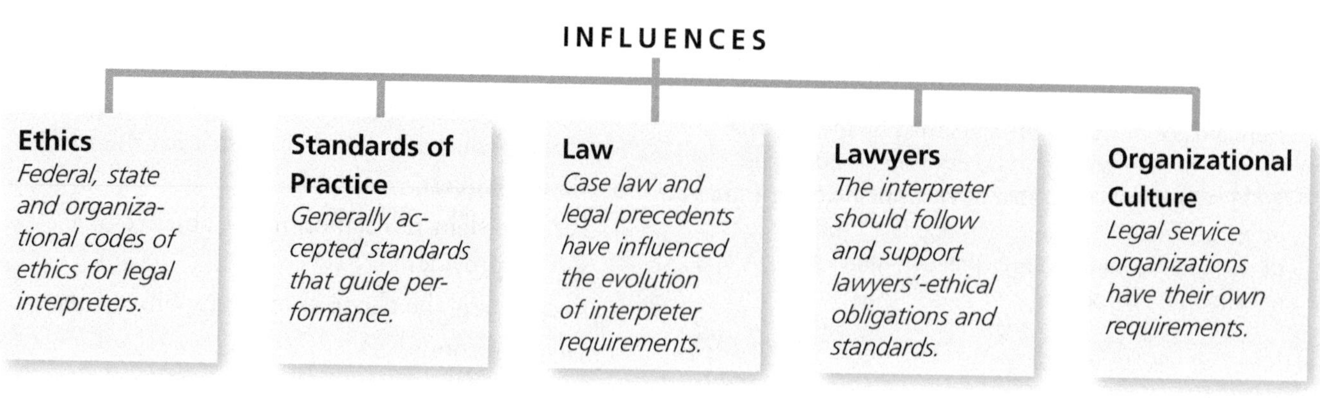

Requirements

Requirements are those things that the interpreter *must* do. In any profession, certain requirements must be followed. Some of the requirements for legal interpreters have been established by law. The interpreter in legal services is responsible for adhering to the following:

- Adhere to the applicable code of ethics (discussed below).

- Clarify the role of the legal interpreter.

- Ensure that speakers communicate directly with each other (rather than speaking to the interpreter).

- Respect the lawyer's ethical requirements.

- Adhere to the policies of the individual legal services provider.

- Interpret everything that is said. Do not summarize, add to or change the message.

- Withdraw from any assignment that exceeds the interpreter's capacity to interpret accurately.

- Refuse all gifts and compensation from either side beyond the agreed-on remuneration for interpreting.

- Refrain from socializing with the client outside the encounter.

- Promote conditions that facilitate accurate interpreting (for example, adjust the seating arrangements or request more time to review documents before sight translating them).

- Notify all individuals immediately of any possible conflict of interest before the assignment or if one develops (*e.g.*, the interpreter may know or be related to the client or the opposing party or may have had prior involvement with the case).

- Notify all individuals about any impediment to accurate interpreting, including unclear speech, ambiguous statements, background noise that interferes with audibility, distractions, and inappropriate behaviors.

- Not answer questions that might violate the interpreter's code of ethics.

- Withdraw if any events occur that violate the interpreter's ethical obligations (guidance on how to develop an awareness of these ethical obligations is discussed below). Note that the interpreter's ethical obligations derive from both the interpreter and lawyer's codes of ethics.

Professionalism

One purpose of supporting requirements and procedures is to demonstrate the interpreter's **professionalism**.

Procedures

Procedures assist the interpreter in executing the assignment appropriately. They are less restrictive than requirements, and may vary according to the individual case. In general, the following procedures will be necessary or useful:

- Prior to the assignment, obtain: name and address of the agency, contact name and phone number, general information about the client and case, date, time and location of the appointment, written documents that may be sight translated, the language/dialect/regional variation, and sensitive information (for example, the client's ethnicity may be relevant).

- Where possible, become familiar with the case before the appointment.

- Arrive 15 minutes before the appointment.

- Adopt professional dress and conduct.

- On arrival, announce yourself as the interpreter and request the contact person.

- On meeting the legal services provider and client, especially the first time, engage in a professional introduction that lays down clear parameters for the interpreted session, inviting questions.

- Ask if there is any information that you should know.

- Determine whether you can understand and adequately interpret the client's language/dialect/regional variations.

- Request, and facilitate, direct communication between the legal services provider and client (so that they do not speak to the interpreter).

- Adopt an unobtrusive position and demeanor.

- Allow the legal services provider and client to end the session. Do not leave until the session is terminated.

- Do not remain alone with the **client.**

- Remain with the legal services provider after the session if he or she has additional questions.

- If you are the sole interpreter for the session, after about one and half hours of interpreting, or whenever you feel tired or lack focus, politely request a break of at least 10 to 15 minutes to ensure accurate interpreting.

- Withdraw from the assignment if the interpreter is being treated inappropriately (for example, if there is rudeness, verbal abuse, any threat to the interpreter or frequent criticism of the interpreter's accuracy).

The Importance of Procedures

Even if procedures are less strict than requirements, they should be followed wherever possible.

Practices

Interpreting practices guide the interpreter. They are not official guidelines but generally accepted practices. They guide the interpreter in how to perform the job well and to meet professional standards in the interpreting and legal fields.

While interpreting for legal services providers, the interpreter should respect standard professional practices. Many of these will be discussed in more detail in Unit II but are summarized below as an introduction.

- Prepare for the session by researching/studying the appropriate terminology.

- Interpret in consecutive mode.

- Perform sight translation as needed.

- Use direct speech (first person: "I really need an attorney"), not reported speech ("He said he needs an attorney").

- In languages with formal and informal forms for "you," address all speakers except minors using the more formal register.

- Exhibit a warm yet professional demeanor.

- Try to avoid eye contact while interpreting, to discourage speakers from addressing the interpreter; the attorney and client should speak directly to each other.

- Manage the flow of communication, directing speakers to pause or slow down as needed.

- Request repetition when necessary.

- Request clarification if the interpreter fails to understand a term or phrase.

- Report barriers to communication (*e.g.*, culturally bound linguistic terms or the lack of an equivalent phrase or concept in the target language).

- Invite speakers to check for understanding where appropriate. (Guidance on how to do so is provided in Unit II on linguistic mediation.)

- Withdraw from the assignment if the interpreter fails to understand three or four terms near the beginning of the interview, unless they are very technical terms within a specialized area of law. Withdrawing from the assignment is necessary to ensure the safety of the client and the legal outcome. This also protects the interpreter and attorney from possible liability.

Professional Introductions and the Pre-Conference

One of the most important procedures involved in executing one's work as a legal interpreter will be performing a professional introduction at every encounter. Most legal services providers and clients are still unfamiliar with the practices of professional interpreters, and the interpreter's introduction is an opportunity to lay down clear parameters for how the interpreted session will proceed.

This introduction, however, should be brief and should include both the attorney and the attorney's client. On some occasions, a private pre-conference with the attorney may be possible. During a pre-conference, the interpreter may offer more detailed parameters for how the interpreted session may best proceed. The attorney may also ask questions, offer helpful information about the case, give the interpreter documents to be sight translated or explain some of the technical terms that might used.

Guidance on how to execute a successful pre-conference is discussed in Unit II.

Often, however, a pre-conference will not be possible. At a minimum, a professional introduction will be necessary. Allowing the interpreter to highlight how the session will proceed can help make the session go smoothly. Ideally, the interpreter's introduction *at a minimum* would include the following components.

- Name and agency ("Good morning, my name is Susan Cheng. I'm an interpreter with the Community Legal Interpreter Bank.").
- "Everything said will be interpreted, exactly as it is said."*
- "Everything will be kept confidential. The notes I take during the session will be left with the attorney."
- "Please speak directly to each other, not to me. Try to act as if I were not present."
- "Please speak in the first person: for example, please try to say 'I need legal advice,' and not,

'Tell her I need legal advice.' " [Use best judgment about whether it is necessary to explain what "first person" means.]

- "Please use simple language as much as possible and explain everything clearly and slowly."

If time permits, the interpreter may then add other helpful elements. For example, the interpreter may wish to say:

- "Please pause after one or two sentences so I can interpret accurately."
- "Please be aware that I will need to take a break if the interview lasts longer than one or two hours."

In their introduction some interpreters find it useful to request that clients or providers refrain from saying anything they would not wish to be interpreted, since the interpreter is obligated to interpret everything said during the encounter.

The interpreter should make the initial introduction to the lawyer or legal services provider, then to the client.

Clarifying the Interpreter's Role

Even if there is no time for a formal pre-conference, it may be wise to alert the lawyer to the interpreter's professional role. Lawyers may have an expectation that they can appeal to the interpreter for personal opinions about the client or about cultural issues. For example, many lawyers ask interpreters about the client's understanding of the case and whether a client is competent or is telling the truth. To avoid this type of situation, the interpreter may:

- Explain to the lawyer that if s/he wishes to speak to the interpreter as an expert on language, s/he may do so during a separate session before or after the interpreted encounter (*i.e.*, at a pre-conference or post-session).
- Make clear that outside the session the interpreter will be able to discuss only in *broad and general terms* the type of linguistic-cultural misunderstandings that can arise and that it is usually preferable for the attorney to direct such questions to the client, not the interpreter.
- If the attorney asks for cultural advice, explain that, in general, legal interpreters are asked to

---

* This does not imply that the interpreter will interpret literally; interpreting everything "exactly as said" means that the interpreter will interpret accurately and completely. The goal is to interpret for *meaning*.

avoid making broad statements about culture, even outside the interpreted encounter. The reason for doing so is that when talking about culture it is easy for interpreters to fall into cultural traps and stereotype a client. There is no such thing as a single "culture" or a magic list of characteristics that applies to everyone from a certain country.

- The interpreter must be clear that he or she is not a "cultural expert" and confine her remarks to those that will facilitate overcoming linguistic barriers, including barriers caused by cultural misunderstandings.

Because it is a common expectation among legal service providers that the interpreter should speak on cultural issues, it may be helpful to emphasize that the interpreter is not a cultural expert because: (a) he or she is not a trained anthropologist specialized in a particular culture; and (b) every person is an individual. Any individual's life experience, education, personal value and beliefs, degree of acculturation, family background and so forth will influence that individual's responses to a given situation. Thus, the interpreter is never an expert on a client. Only the client is an expert on him- or herself. Only the client can speak with confidence about his or her cultural beliefs.

A Note on Positioning

With the exception of sign language interpreters, there is no general rule or consensus in legal interpreting about an "ideal position." The interpreter should however position him- or herself in a location that is unobtrusive in order not to draw attention to the interpreter. Allow the focus of the interview to be direct communication between the client and the legal services provider. The interpreter must also be able to hear all speakers.

One preferred position (if possible) is for the interpreter to sit beside and slightly behind the client, allowing the provider and client to face each other. This position is helpful because:

- The interpreter will be unobtrusive (an ethical requirement).
- The interpreter will not be too close to the legal services provider; seeing the interpreter

next to a lawyer could, and often does, intimidate the client.

- Taking a more prominent position inadvertently encourages the client to communicate with the interpreter instead of the legal services provider.

- Remaining beside and slightly behind the client helps the interpreter to avoid eye contact with other individuals while interpreting. This facilitates direct communication between the legal services provider and client and allows the interpreter to concentrate on interpreting accurately.

The classic position adopted by many interpreters is the triangle, which is often a problematic position. Rather than promoting direct communication, the triangle often promotes the following interactions:

- The client and lawyer tend to look at the interpreter, not each other.

- The relationship of trust is more easily built between the interpreter and the client, rather than between the client and the legal services provider.

- The client and provider are more likely to slip into third person (indirect speech).

To promote *direct communication* between the client and provider.

Codes *of* Ethics *and* Professional Responsibility

Demonstrate a sound understanding of relevant codes of ethics

Ethical Dilemmas

Ethics are important. They tell us what to do in difficult situations. For example, in situations like the following, what would you do?

What Would *You* Do?

After an interpreted session in a legal clinic regarding a landlord-tenant dispute

Interpreter: (leaving the session). Thank you. Have a good day!

Mrs. Sanchez: (speaking in Spanish) Please, just a moment, I have a question.

Interpreter: Would you like me to ask the lawyer to come back, Mrs. Sanchez? I'm afraid I'm not authorized to answer legal questions.

Mrs. Sanchez: No, no, nothing like that. (whispers) It's just... I didn't tell the lawyer everything about my situation. Actually, my husband and I—well, we're not really married. But that doesn't matter, right? And the children, they're not his. I don't know how the lawyer will take it if he finds that out, after we have been working together so long. Do you think he will get upset with me if I tell him now?

What Would *You* Do?

During a session regarding an appeal of denial of benefits for Medical Assistance and other refugee benefits

Mr. Kabamba: (leans over and smiles, whispers to the interpreter in French) I'm glad they have no idea about my second wife in Africa.

Interpreter: (starts to interpret into English) I'm glad they—

Mr. Kabamba (angry, in French) Stop, what are you saying! I didn't want you to interpret that to the lawyer!

This unit offers practical guidance on ethical decision-making.

Codes of Ethics for Legal Interpreters

A code of ethics is a set of principles adopted by a profession to govern the conduct and decision-making of its members. Ethics represent the strictest set of rules in any profession. They support professional integrity.

Codes of Ethics have been adopted for court interpreters through professional associations and the federal and state court systems. Case law and legal analysis based on established judicial procedures and requirements have also influenced the profession's ethical guidelines. Although the codes are generally rather similar, a few subtle differences may exist. While some state court codes of ethics may include lengthy or brief commentaries, some do not. These codes apply to legal interpreters in general, although how to apply the ethical canons outside the courtroom may differ slightly. See the Resources section of this manual for examples of various codes of ethics and conduct for legal interpreters. Examples of such codes include:

- **FEDERAL COURTS:** Federally certified interpreters who interpret in the federal courts follow a national code of ethics.

- **STATE COURTS:** The *Model Code of Professional Responsibility* was created by the National Center for State Courts (NCSC) and its Consortium for State Court Interpreter Certification. This Code has been adopted or adapted by the Consortium's member states.

- **NAJIT:** The NAJIT Code of Ethics and Professional Responsibility was developed by NAJIT, the U.S. legal interpreting profession's only national association. Thus, this code was created *by* legal interpreters based on legal requirements and standards for legal interpreters.

- **INTERPRETER SERVICES:** Many commercial or nonprofit interpreter services have also created codes to govern the interpreters that these agencies send out to courts, legal services providers and other assignments such as conference, escort, government and/or community interpreting. These ethics typically are not directed at legal interpreting only, but at all areas of interpreting for which the agency offers interpreter services, including legal.

- **OTHER ENTITIES:** Other codes have been developed by individual states or state courts and by local (county/municipal) public and private agencies.

A Model Code

Ethics are the foundation of a profession. No member of an established profession can function effectively without a set of ethical principles to guide his or her behavior. This is also true for the legal interpreter.

When working inside the courtroom, the court interpreter should be given a code of ethics to adhere to. The legal interpreter who works only outside the courtroom may not have a code of ethics to follow. Yet it is vital that *all* legal interpreters adhere to a set of ethical principles already established for legal interpreters.

For the purposes of this training program, the authors include two documents. The first is a list the 10 canons excerpted from NCSC Model Code of Professional Responsibility for Interpreters in the Judiciary. (A "code of professional responsibility," in this context, is equivalent to a code of ethics.) All legal interpreters should be aware of this document because it may be the most widely followed code of ethics for legal interpreters in the U.S. The complete NCSC model code with its commentary is available at **www.ncsconline.org**.

The second document was prepared by the Advisory Board for this curriculum. That document contains standards of practice that are intended to guide interpreters on *how to adhere to the NCSC canons while interpreting for legal services*. It includes specific examples of situations that the interpreter will have to consider. While these documents were created for interpreters who work with legal services providers, interpreters who work in almost any legal setting outside the courtroom can use them.

There are several reasons for knowing about and supporting the NCSC code:

- This set of model rules currently has the widest formal application of any code of ethics or conduct for legal interpreters in the U.S., including most members of the NCSC Consortium, which currently has 40 member states.

- The NCSC Code has influenced the profession of legal interpreting perhaps more than any other single code of ethics.

- Its principles are clear and straightforward.

- The NCSC code represents, in its principles and commentary, a discourse on the ethics of court interpreting that is widely agreed on by U.S. experts in the legal interpreting field and by legal professionals.

Created by an advisory group, the NCSC Code represents input from judges, lawyers, court administrators and state and federally certified judiciary interpreters. Its aim, as articulated by the advisory group that developed it, was to lay out a model code that could be adapted to courts anywhere in the country and serve as a reference work, offering a basis for the education and training of court interpreters and other legal professionals.

However, the ethical canons themselves are not sufficient; each interpreter must also know how to adapt those canons to real-life situations. Each interpreter will also have to exhibit sound judgment when applying the canons.

The 10 canons of the NCSC code were adapted in 2006 for interpreters who serve victims of domestic violence (Uekert *et al* 2006:180-189) (see Table 1). That document was published by NCSC and the National Institute of Justice in a report entitled *Serving Limited English Proficient (LEP) Battered Women: A National Survey of the Courts' Capacity to Provide Protection Orders*. It is available at **www.ncjrs.gov** (see pp. 180-186). In this document, the NCSC code was adapted to help interpreters better understand their role outside the courtroom when interpreting in protection-from-abuse or sexual assault proceedings.

TABLE 1:
Canons of the NCSC Model Code of Professional Responsibility for Interpreters in the Judiciary

Canon 1: **Accuracy and Completeness**	Interpreters shall render a complete and accurate interpretation or sight translation, without altering, omitting, or adding anything to what is stated or written, and without explanation.
Canon 2: **Representation of Qualifications**	Interpreters shall accurately and completely represent their certifications, training, and pertinent experience.
Canon 3: **Impartiality and Avoidance of Conflict of Interest**	Interpreters shall be impartial and unbiased and shall refrain from conduct that may give an appearance of bias. Interpreters shall disclose any real or perceived conflict of interest.
Canon 4: **Professional Demanor**	Interpreters shall conduct themselves in a manner consistent with the dignity of the court and shall be as unobtrusive as possible.
Canon 5: **Confidentiality**	Interpreters shall protect the confidentiality of all privileged and other confidential information.
Canon 6: **Restriction of Public Comment**	Interpreters shall not publicly discuss, report, or offer an opinion concerning a matter in which they are or have been engaged, even when that information is not privileged or required by law to be confidential.
Canon 7: **Scope of Practice**	Interpreters shall limit themselves to interpreting or translating, and shall not give legal advice, express personal opinions to individuals for whom they are interpreting, or engage in any other activities which may be construed to constitute a service other than interpreting or translating while serving as an interpreter.
Canon 8: **Assessing and Reporting Impediments to Performance**	Interpreters shall assess at all times their ability to deliver their services. When interpreters have any reservation about their ability to satisfy an assignment competently, they shall immediately convey that reservation to the appropriate judicial authority.
Canon 9: **Duty to Report Ethical Violations**	Interpreters shall report to the proper judicial authority any effort to impede their compliance with any law, any provision of this code, or any other official policy governing court interpreting and legal translating.
Canon 10: **Professional Development**	Interpreters shall continually improve their skills and knowledge and advance the profession through activities such as professional training and education, and interaction with colleagues and specialists in related fields.

Applying Ethics *and* Standards *of* Practice

UNIT I, OBJECTIVE 3

Demonstrate the correct application of a code of ethics and standards of practice to ethical dilemmas and simulated encounters

Standards of Practice

Ethics are the rules of a profession. They are strict, rigid and formal.

> **Standards of Practice**
>
> A clear set of formal guidelines that show those who practice a profession how to execute their duties and uphold ethical requirements.

Standards of practice are the guidelines of a profession. They are more flexible. They show the interpreters how to uphold a code of ethics and conduct themselves in a professional manner while adhering to standards that maintain the quality and integrity of the profession.

Ethic rules show the interpreter what to do. Standards show them how to do it. For this reason, it is common to see standards of practice listed under headings taken from the basic principles or "canons" of a code of ethics.

Approximately 40 states have adopted the NCSC Model Code of Professional Responsibility, which constitutes the basis for the standards presented below.

Standards of Practice for Interpreters in Legal Services

These Standards of Practice are designed to complement the National Center for State Court's Model Code of Professional Responsibility for Interpreters in the Judiciary. The canons and commentary are excerpted and modified, with permission, from the Code of Professional Responsibility for Interpreters Serving Limited English Proficiency (LEP) Victims of Domestic Violence. The Canons are essentially the same for all legal interpreters; however these Standards give specific guidance on how to apply the canons when interpreting outside of the courtroom. For in-court proceedings, interpreters are governed by, and must strictly observe, the provisions and commentary of the Code of Professional Responsibility for Interpreters or the relevant code that has been established by the Court in which the interpreter is serving. These Standards are designed to guide the interpreter, support and preserve client confidentiality and the attorney-client privilege, to enhance the relationship between the attorney and the client, and to support the interpreter in maintaining proper boundaries and avoiding misunderstandings and the unauthorized practice of law.

Canon 1: Accuracy and Completeness

Interpreters shall render a complete and accurate interpretation or sight translation, without altering, omitting, or adding anything to what is stated or written, and without explanation.

Commentary:

The interpreter's duty is to assist the lawyer in putting the Deaf, Hard of Hearing, or Limited English Proficient (LEP) person (the client*) on an equal footing with those who understand spoken English. The interpreter accomplishes this by ensuring that conversations and discussions in spoken English are interpreted accurately for a client; and ensuring that information and discussions in the client's language are interpreted accurately for the English-speaking participants in the process.

Therefore, interpreters are obligated to apply their best skills and judgment to preserve faithfully the meaning of what is said, including the style or

---

* In these Standards of Practice, the deaf, hard of hearing, or Limited English Proficient person will generally be referred to as the client.

register of speech. Verbatim, "word for word," or literal oral interpretations are not appropriate if they distort the meaning of the source language. It is common for judges and attorneys to request the interpreter to interpret verbatim. What they mean is that the interpreter should interpret everything exactly as said, using the closest natural equivalent. The choice of terminology ("verbatim") shows a lack of understanding about the terms of art of the interpreting profession. A request to interpret "verbatim" does not mean that the judge or attorney expects the interpreter to interpret word-for-word when the result would be misleading or nonsensical.

Every spoken statement, even if it appears non-responsive, obscene, rambling, or incoherent should be interpreted. This includes apparent misstatements. The interpretation of all spoken statements will help the legal services provider more clearly understand the client's philosophy, attitude, and level of understanding. The provider will base her legal advice, in part, on these observations of not only what the client is saying but how she is saying it, and will rely on an accurate interpretation to form the legal opinion.

Maintaining transparency (interpreting every utterance for both parties) is a critical element in ensuring accuracy and completeness. This includes every utterance by the interpreter. If the interpreter asks the provider to pause more often, she must interpret that request (and any response to that request) to the client. A lack of transparency will leave one or both parties feeling excluded from part of the session and will raise suspicions that the interpreter is not rendering a complete interpretation.

Interpreters should convey the emotional emphasis of the client without re-enacting or mimicking the speaker's emotions or dramatic gestures. Sign language interpreters, however, must employ visual cues as required by the visual language they are interpreting. Sign language interpreters, therefore, should ensure that providers do not confuse these elements of the visual language with inappropriate interpreter conduct.

Interpreters should not interject their own words, phrases, or expressions as a substitute for what is actually said. Interpreters should not summarize statements of the legal services provider or the client.

The interpreter should immediately interrupt if she is unable to keep up with the speaker or needs to consult reference materials. If the need arises to explain an interpreting problem or a linguistic barrier in order to facilitate communication, the interpreter should ask for the provider's permission to do so and interpret that request and response. If a discussion of the problem or barrier becomes necessary, the interpreter should prompt *the provider* to explore the barrier and to check for understanding. The interpreter should not assume the responsibility of clarification, but assist the provider in seeking clarification.

The obligation to preserve accuracy includes the interpreter's duty to correct any error of interpretation as soon as it is discovered. The interpreter should interrupt the session immediately to correct the error and interpret the interruption for both the legal services provider and the client.

Examples:
- Interpret even fillers like "um," "er," etc.
- Advise all parties before the session begins that *everything said will be interpreted.*
- Do not "tidy up" or "improve" language: for example "Dunno" is similar to "I don't know" but it gives the attorney a very different impression of the speaker.
- Do not try to make a sophisticated client sound unsophisticated or vice versa.
- Never simplify a message, even if the listener does not understand it. When the client is confused, it is up to the legal services provider to simplify or explain, not the interpreter.
- If the client seems confused and this lack of understanding could have serious consequences (but apparently has not been noticed by the attorney), the interpreter may signal to both parties that, "there appears to be a breakdown in communication." However, it is up to the attorney to resolve the problem.

Canon 2: Representation of Qualifications

Interpreters shall accurately and completely represent their certifications, training, and pertinent experience.

Commentary:

Acceptance of a legal interpreting job by an interpreter is an implicit statement that the interpreter possesses adequate linguistic competency and interpreting skills for a legal setting. It is therefore essential that interpreters present a complete and truthful account of their training, certification, and experience prior to providing interpreting services. An interpreter should immediately notify the provider and the Deaf, Hard of Hearing, or LEP individual if the interpreter determines that his or her skills are not adequate for the assignment.

Examples:

- Do not claim to be certified if you hold only a training certificate. Interpreters must never misrepresent their credentials.

- If you are certified, be sure to state what entity issued your certification. It makes a difference whether Federal Courts, NAJIT or a particular state court certifies you. Some testing standards differ from state to state.

- If you were certified by a language services agency, do not represent this as certification but as a *credential* issued to you by the relevant agency.

- Do not claim to be a translator unless you are fully trained and experienced in the field of legal translation, hold credentials in the field and preferably hold ATA translation certification.

Canon 3: Impartiality and Avoidance of Conflict of Interest

Interpreters shall be impartial and unbiased and shall refrain from conduct that may give an appearance of bias. Interpreters shall disclose any real or perceived conflict of interest.

Commentary:

The interpreter working within the attorney-client relationship is acting as an agent of the attorney. Thus, the interpreter must act in accordance with the attorney's ethical requirements regarding conflicts of interest. These requirements may differ from the requirements in other settings.

The interpreter should strive for professional detachment and avoid any conduct that presents the appearance of bias against or favoritism toward any of the parties. During the course of the case, interpreters should not hold conversations with potential witnesses, attorneys, or friends or relatives of the client or any other party, except as required in the discharge of interpreting duties. Verbal and non-verbal displays of personal attitudes, prejudices, emotions, or opinions should be avoided. Interpreters should use their judgment when interpreting for especially vulnerable clients, including children and victims of crime. With such clients, interpreters should strive to appear professional but caring or gentle to assist the provider in developing a trusting relationship with the client.

An interpreter should not accept an assignment if the interpreter is currently interpreting for the opposing party in a legal setting. If the interpreter has previously provided interpretation for either the client or any other party in the case (in any setting), or if the interpreter has a personal relationship with anyone involved in the case, the interpreter must disclose that information to both the legal services provider and the client to permit a determination whether a conflict of interest exists. If, during the course of the case, the interpreter discovers a potential conflict, it must be immediately disclosed to both the legal services provider and the client to permit a determination of whether a conflict exists.

An interpreter must preserve a strictly professional relationship with the Deaf, Hard of Hearing, or LEP individual for whom he or she is interpreting. An interpreter must neither encourage nor discourage a client with regard to any issues discussed. The interpreter must not engage in conversations with the client, except as required in the discharge of interpreting duties. An interpreter should prudently and with sensitivity discourage a client's personal attachment or dependence upon the interpreter. An interpreter should not accept any gifts or payment from the client or others beyond the interpreter's standard fee, to avoid the appearance of bias or impropriety. If the client develops a personal dependence on the interpreter, the interpreter should disclose that relationship to the legal service provider. Such dependency may create a conflict of interest for the interpreter.

If the client develops a personal dependence on the interpreter, the interpreter should not accept any other interpreting assignments related to the case, including interpreting for the court or for any other party in the case. Such advocacy and dependency creates a conflict of interest for the interpreter, and the interpreter must reveal that conflict to the legal service provider and to the client.

Examples:

- **Do not give advice,** legal or otherwise.
- Do not provide personal opinions.
- Direct the parties to speak to each other, not the interpreter.
- Do not carry on side conversations with either the legal services provider or the client. This action could jeopardize impartiality and transparency and affect the attorney-client relationship.
- If you know the client personally, you must inform the legal services provider immediately that there may be a possible conflict of interest. Offer to withdraw. Remain to interpret only if urged to do so by all present and if the interpreter is certain that he or she is able to interpret impartially.
- Maintain neutrality even when the legal services provider or client is upset, but do not adopt a neutral voice. Instead, render the tone of the speaker's voice without mimicking. Remember that a neutral tone of voice would not convey the speaker's meaning and intent. Maintaining neutrality means that the interpreter reflects the emotions of the speaker but does not allow his or her own feelings to interfere with interpreting.
- Do not interject personal biases or beliefs or allow them to influence the interpreted message.
- Decline any assignment about which the interpreter has very strong biases or feelings (*e.g.,* if the interpreter was sexually assaulted, she may wish to avoid rape cases).
- Avoid disclosing personal information, particularly to the client, even when asked common questions, for example, "Are you married? Do you have children? Do you go to church? Where do you live? Can I have your phone number in case I need to relay something to the attorney?"

Canon 4: Professional Demeanor

Interpreters shall conduct themselves in a professional manner and should be as unobtrusive as possible.

Commentary:

Interpreters working within the attorney-client context will generally work outside of the courtroom. Interpreters should know and observe the established protocols, rules, and procedures relating to interpreting services, including agency specific policies and the ethical requirements of the organization for which those services are rendered. An interpreter should work without drawing undue or inappropriate attention to herself and should dress in a manner that is consistent with the nature of the assignment. Interpreters should avoid personal or professional conduct that discredits the interpreting profession.

Interpreters should dress professionally for all assignments. For interviews conducted within the legal services provider's office, business casual is usually acceptable. However, if the session is to take place at another location or at the court, the interpreter should dress professionally. If the interpreter has any questions about attire, he or she should contact the provider for clarification.

Examples:

- Arrive 15 minutes early.
- Arrive prepared.
- Wherever possible, conduct a pre-conference with the attorney prior to the first meeting with a client.

- Show professionalism, respect and cultural sensitivity towards all individuals for whom you are interpreting.
- Use the formal mode of address in languages where one exists (except for children).
- Address individuals by their last names, using appropriate titles, *e.g.*, Mr., Mrs., Attorney, etc. (except for children: address children by their first names, since otherwise they may be confused).
- Dress professionally. Avoid sandals, jeans, shorts, open-toed shoes, flip-flops, sneakers, revealing and tight or casual clothing (even if some legal services providers dress in this manner).
- Remain as unobtrusive as possible.
- Use first person (direct speech) at all times where appropriate, except when performing linguistic mediation (linguistic mediation is discussed in Unit II).
- Remain composed, even if other persons are excited or upset.

Canon 5: Confidentiality

Interpreters shall protect the confidentiality of all privileged and other confidential information.

Commentary:

Interpreters working within the attorney-client context are responsible for adhering to the attorney's ethical duty to maintain client confidentiality. Interpreters must not disclose information deemed confidential by statute, case law, attorney ethics rules, or court rule or policy. Any and all information disclosed by the client, including the name of the client may be considered confidential and should not be disclosed. The interpreter should consult the legal service provider before disclosing any information to anyone other than the legal services provider or the client (including family members or friends of the client).

The interpreter, acting solely as a professional interpreter, is included within the attorney-client privilege. This privilege protects the attorney and the interpreter from the possibility of being subject to a subpoena, or forced to testify, about the information disclosed by the client. The privilege protects the client, allowing her/him to talk freely with her/his legal services provider. The privilege is owned by the client, and is eternal. The client is the only person with the authority to waive the privilege.

It is essential that the interpreter not disclose to a third party any information learned in the course of communications with the attorney and/or client, as doing so may place the client in jeopardy. The interpreter must not reveal even general information such as the name or address of the client, as that may jeopardize confidentiality, attorney-client privilege, and/or the safety of the client. This would be a serious breach of interpreter ethics and could result in litigation against the interpreter, loss of interpreter certification or accreditation, loss of the legal service provider's license, and untold harm to the client.

In the event that an interpreter becomes aware of information that suggests imminent harm to someone or relates to a crime being or about to be committed, or if a client asks the interpreter to violate the law or to discuss the case outside of the interpreting context, the interpreter should immediately contact the legal service provider for advice.

If the interpreter has any questions about what information is confidential and/or privileged, he or she should err on the side of caution and assume that the information is privileged. The interpreter should request advice from the legal services provider, and defer to her, regarding any disclosure of information.

Examples:

- Leave any notes taken during the session with the attorney.
- The only notes that the interpreter may carry away are those that list new legal terms, case numbers for the interpreter's reference, or other information that belongs to the interpreter alone.
- Uphold confidentiality and attorney-client privilege at all times. If the interpreter were to be required by law to break confidentiality or violate the attorney-client privilege (for example, if the interpreter receives a subpoena to testify in court), consult first with the attorney involved in the case. Subpoenas are a request for information. The attorney can determine if it is appropriate to challenge the subpoena.

- Avoid speaking with clients outside the session. Depending what is said, speaking with clients out of the lawyer's presence could result in accusations of the unauthorized practice of law, particularly if the interpreter's statements are construed—or misconstrued—as advice. Other risky implications include the possibility that such conversations are not covered by attorney-client privilege, because an opposing party's attorney might then subpoena the interpreter to testify about such conversations in court, potentially putting a case in jeopardy.

Canon 6: Restriction of Public Comment

Interpreters shall not publicly discuss, report, or offer an opinion concerning a matter in which they are or have been engaged, even when that information is not privileged or required by law to be confidential.

Commentary:

Interpreters must avoid speaking to the media or any other person or entity about the facts of a case, including the name and characteristics of any parties to the case, and should not voice an opinion about the veracity of the parties, evidence or possible outcome of the case.

Interpreters providing services in any legal setting should be careful to refrain from repeating or disclosing *any* information about the case, including the names of the parties and the nature of the case, regardless of whether that information is privileged or otherwise deemed confidential.

Examples:

- Do not confirm or deny information about a case for the media, even if that information was discussed in open court.

- Do not offer opinions on cases in which you were professionally involved.

Canon 7: Scope of Practice

Interpreters shall limit themselves to interpreting or translating, and shall not give legal advice, express personal opinions to individuals for whom they are interpreting, or engage in any other activities which may be construed to constitute a service other than interpreting or translating.

Commentary:

The interpreter's only role is to enable others to communicate; therefore the interpreter's activities are limited to interpreting or translating. Interpreters should refrain from initiating communications while interpreting unless such communications are necessary to ensure an accurate and faithful interpretation. Interpreters may be required to initiate communications when they find it necessary to seek assistance in performing their duties. Examples of such circumstances include seeking clarification if the interpreter is unable to understand or express a word or thought, requesting permission to clarify an unfamiliar regionalism, seeking permission to consult a bilingual dictionary or other resource, requesting speakers to moderate their rate of communication or repeat or rephrase a statement, correcting interpreting errors, or notifying the legal service provider when the interpreter has reservations about his/her own ability to satisfy an assignment competently. To signify that the interpreter is speaking personally and not interpreting, the interpreter should refer to himself or herself in the third person; *e.g.* "The interpreter requests …" The interpreter must also interpret the entire discussion.

Attorneys have made clear that they do not appreciate receiving legal advice from interpreters.

For example, one attorney reports: "Comments from the interpreter about how to conduct settlement negotiations are truly not welcome."

An interpreter should not independently explain the purpose of forms, services, or otherwise act as counselors or advisors. The interpreter may sight translate language on a form for a client in the presence of a legal services provider, but must not explain the form or its purpose for the individual.

The legal service provider is ethically bound to zealously represent and advocate for the client. The interpreter should not attempt to undertake this duty; as such actions are likely to confuse the client. In fact, actions such as explaining a form, giving advice about what actions to take, or giving general information about the legal system may constitute the Unauthorized Practice of Law. The interpreter could be found liable for such actions. Such activities could also implicate the legal service provider, under whose supervision the interpretation is being provided, leading to sanction against the attorney. The interpreter should interpret any question or request of the client to the legal service provider and then interpret the provider's response, no matter how simple the question appears or how knowledgeable the interpreter may be about the subject.

Examples:

- Never express a personal opinion or belief.

- Never make suggestions or recommendations, or give advice.

- Never perform advocacy on behalf of the client for whom you are interpreting.

- Do not answer a client's questions; instead, refer questions to the attorney or legal staff.

- Decline sight translations if they are beyond the scope of your expertise, too technical or so unreasonably long that it would be difficult to render an accurate and complete sight translation without consulting a dictionary at every step.

- Private questions by the attorney should be addressed outside the session, preferably during a pre-conference between the attorney and the interpreter.

- Avoid "culture brokering" or cultural mediation.

- Do not perform services other than interpreting for clients or legal services providers.

- ***Never undertake any acts that could be construed as the practice of law,*** for example, by making recommendations or suggestions to a client, or by expressing opinions or comments on a case or explaining a legal form or legal concept. It is unlawful to practice law without a license.

- If the client approaches the interpreter separately or privately to request help with a problem (this is extremely common), do not offer information; instead, immediately refer the client back to the attorney or other legal services staff so that they, not the interpreter, may provide referrals to appropriate agencies that can assist the client.

Canon 8: Assessing and Reporting Impediments to Performance

Interpreters shall assess at all times their ability to deliver their services. When interpreters have any reservation about their ability to satisfy an assignment competently, the interpreter shall immediately convey that reservation to the person or entity retaining the interpreter.

Commentary:

If the communication mode or language of the non-English-speaking person cannot be readily interpreted, if the subject matter is likely to exceed the interpreter's skills, or if after starting an assignment, the interpreter believes s/he cannot perform competently for any reason, the interpreter should notify the legal service provider immediately.

Interpreters should also report any environmental or physical limitation that impedes the ability to deliver interpreting services adequately (*e.g.*, outside noise interferes with the interpreter's ability to hear or be heard, more than one person at a time is speaking, or individuals are speaking too rapidly). Sign language interpreters must ensure that they can both see and convey the full range of visual language elements that are necessary for communication, including facial expressions and body movement, as well as hand gestures. (Spoken language interpreters, however, should not interpret body language or gestures.)

Whenever possible, interpreters are encouraged to inquire into the nature and topic of the interpreting assignment before accepting the assignment. This enables interpreters to match their professional qualifications, skills, and experience to potential assignments appropriately and assess the interpreter's ability to perform interpreting duties competently.

Interpreters may request, preferably during a pre-conference, that the legal services provider begin the session with a few basic questions which will allow the interpreter to determine that the client can understand the interpreter. The interpreter should not conduct this questioning as a separate side conversation, but should maintain transparency at all times. The interpreter should suggest that the provider ask the client, after the preliminary questions, if the client can understand the interpreter easily.

Interpreters should notify the legal services provider of any perceived or actual personal bias relating to any aspect of the assignment. For example, an interpreter who has been the victim of a sexual assault may wish to be excused from interpreting in cases involving similar offenses, and a person accused or convicted of domestic abuse should not interpret for a domestic violence victim.

Examples:

- If there is noise or other interference that impedes performance, let the legal service provider know that you are having difficulties hearing or concentrating.

- If there may be conflicts or biases because the interpreter and the client are from different ethnic/tribal/religious groups—or the interpreter comes from the same very small group as the client—report the potential conflict and allow the attorney and client to decide how to handle the situation.

- Withdraw if the client's language/dialect/regional variation is not a good match for the interpreter's skills. Important nuances could be missed, or idioms might be misinterpreted.

Canon 9: Duty to Report Ethical Violations

Interpreters shall report to the legal service provider any effort to impede their compliance with any law, any provision of this code, or any other official policy governing legal interpreting and translating.

Commentary:

Users of interpreting services may inadvertently ask or expect interpreters to perform duties or engage in activities that violate the provisions of this code or other laws, regulations, or policies governing interpreters. It is incumbent upon the interpreter to inform such persons of an interpreter's professional obligations. If, having been apprised of these obligations, the person persists in demanding that the interpreter engage in prohibited behavior, the interpreter should either speak with the legal service provider's supervising attorney, or should decline to accept further interpreting assignments from that provider. The interpreter should not disclose the details of any request related to the case outside of the attorney-client relationship, as that might breach confidentiality and/or the attorney-client privilege.

Examples:

- If the client repeatedly asks the interpreter to help the client make a decision about her case, the interpreter should report those requests to the legal service provider. The provider will then be able to address any concerns of the client and will not be suspicious of the relationship between the client and the interpreter.

- If the attorney repeatedly asks the interpreter to help a client fill out forms when the attorney is not present, the interpreter should first schedule a meeting with the attorney to discuss the ethical challenges presented. If that does not solve the problem, the interpreter should schedule a meeting with the attorney's supervisor to discuss the situation.

Canon 10: Professional Development

Interpreters shall continually improve their skills and knowledge and advance the profession through activities such as professional training and education, and interaction with colleagues and specialists in related fields.

Commentary:

Interpreters must continually strive to increase their knowledge of the languages they interpret, including past and current trends in technical, vernacular, and regional terminology as well as their application in legal settings.

Interpreters should keep informed of all statutes, rules, and policies that relate to the performance of their professional duties.

Interpreters should seek to elevate the standards of the profession through participation in workshops and professional meetings, interaction with colleagues, and reading current literature in the field.

Interpreters for legal services are encouraged to seek out workshops, trainings, and literature on the legal field to improve their understanding of the legal system and terminology.

Examples:

- Read and occasionally review the interpreter's code of ethics as well as the attorney's code of ethics.

- Build a network of colleagues to consult for linguistic expertise and decisions on ethical choices.

- Attend cultural competence and/or diversity training to identify personal biases that might affect interpreting and develop cultural knowledge to enhance accurate interpreting.

- Read books and articles on legal interpreting to reinforce the knowledge needed.

- Develop study habits, *e.g.*, practice consecutive interpreting or sight translation for a few minutes each day, learn a few new terms each day, or practice memory skills.

- Purchase or build resources such as specialized terminology glossaries, dictionaries and other reference works and make the time to study them.

- Watch court programs or movies on legal issues; read novels and short stories about legal situations.

- Consult other legal interpreters for their recommendations about resources and works to study or events to attend.

- Work on your weaker language through reading, television, radio, practice, language classes, and travel and study in the country where that language is spoken.

- Attend interpreting in-services or seminars where available.

- Join appropriate professional organizations and their listservs, which post announcements about training, books, resources and conferences.

Applying a Code of Ethics

When interpreting for legal services providers, challenging situations may arise that pose ethical dilemmas for the interpreter (and often for the attorney, whether or not he or she is aware of the problem). Some of these situations are minor. Many are serious. All are important.

In general, it is not enough for the interpreter to become familiar with the relevant code of ethics. The interpreter must also be able to decide, often quickly, about how to apply that code to real life. Yet few official documents offer interpreters clear guidance on how to respond to ethical dilemmas. The California Healthcare Interpreting Association (CHIA) developed one example as part of its standards of practice. The relevant portion contains six rules that offer interpreters a road map for analyzing what to do when an ethical dilemma arises. These rules are equally helpful for legal interpreters.

CHIA Guidelines

What is "CHIA"?

The California Healthcare Interpreting Association (CHIA) is one of the two largest healthcare interpreting associations in the country. (The other is the International Medical Interpreters Association, IMIA, based in Massachusetts.)

Why did CHIA create an ethical decision-making protocol?

Many interpreters in health care were confused about how to respect codes of ethics. CHIA established a list of questions to help guide interpreters as they make decisions.

The Guidelines

1. Ask questions to determine whether there is a problem. *[If needed, the interpreter may ask questions silently, in his or her own mind.]*

2. Identify and clearly state the problem, considering the ethical principles that may apply and ranking them in applicability.

3. Clarify personal values as they relate to the problem.

4. Consider alternative actions, including benefits and risks.

5. Decide to carry out the action chosen.

6. Evaluate the outcome and consider what might be done differently next time.

—California Healthcare Interpreting Association
*Available at **www.chiaonline.org***

Unit I
Review

Definitions

Give a definition in your own words of the following:

Legal services:

____

____

____

Certified interpreter:

____

____

____

Legal interpreting:

____

____

____

Multiple Choice

Circle the correct answer.

1. Legal interpreters must follow:

   a. The NAJIT Code of Ethics and Professional Responsibility.

   b. The NCSC Model Code of Professional Responsibility for Interpreters in the Judiciary.

   c. The Federal Court Interpreter Ethics and Protocol.

   d. All of the above.

   e. Any of the above, depending on the venue.

2. If the interpreter, on arriving at a session, finds out that he knows the client, the interpreter should:

   a. Inform the attorney of the possible conflict.

   b. Request to withdraw from the case ("conflict out") if a real or perceived conflict exists.

   c. Stay only if all present strongly request it and the interpreter feels that he or she can be completely impartial.

   d. All of the above.

3. An interpreter working with a legal services provider may:

   a. Let the provider know if the client is telling the truth.

   b. Remind the attorney that if the interpreter is left alone with a client, any conversation between the interpreter and the client may put attorney-client privilege at risk.

   c. Be careful to inform the attorney during the session about all the cultural barriers that are causing problems.

   d. All of the above.

Requirements and procedures

Strike out any items in the list below of requirements and procedures that are *inappropriate* for a legal interpreter.

The interpreter should:

- Present a calm, self-confident, professional demeanor.
- Clarify the role of the legal interpreter.
- Ensure that speakers communicate directly with each other.
- Gracefully decline gifts from clients.
- Refrain from socializing with the client outside the encounter.
- ~~Give information about the client's culture to help the case.~~
- Try to arrive about 15 minutes before the appointment.
- Engage in a professional introduction that lays down clear parameters for the interpreted session.
- ~~Reassure the client that the lawyer is trying to help and is competent.~~
- Continually facilitate direct communication between the lawyer and the client.
- Adopt a non-obtrusive position that facilitates direct communication between the client and legal services provider.
- ~~Answer questions during the session from either the client or attorney (*e.g.*, about a sight translation).~~
- After two hours, politely request a break.

True or False

Circle T for "True" or F for "False"

1. Legal interpreting is part of the profession of court interpreting. T 
2. Legal interpreters may advocate for clients as needed. T 
3. Lawyers may advocate for clients as needed.  F
4. The court interpreter is considered an officer of the court. T F
5. Unlike most court interpreting, attorney-client interviews involve a collaborative relationship (*e.g.*, an attorney tries to help a client). T F
6. Most legal interpreters are certified.  F
7. The code of ethics for the Federal courts is the most widely followed code of ethics for legal interpreters in the U.S. T 
8. If the attorney makes a casual joke that does not make sense in the target language, the interpreter should just ignore/omit the joke and interpret everything else of substance. T 
9. During a professional introduction, the legal interpreter can lay down parameters for how the interpreted session can proceed smoothly.  F

Positioning

What is the purpose of trying to adopt an effective position when interpreting for an attorney-client interview?

____

____

____

____

____

Why is it usually helpful to refrain from making eye contact when performing legal interpreting outside the courtroom?

____

____

____

____

____

Legal, Court and Community Interpreting

What are some of the differences between court interpreting and non-courtroom legal interpreting?

____

____

____

____

____

____

What are some of the differences between legal and community interpreting?

____

____

____

____

____

Give three specific examples of non-courtroom legal interpreting that you might perform (_e.g._, interpreting for an attorney at a domestic violence center, for a Board hearing at a school or for a nonprofit agency that provides legal services in employment law). Do not use the examples just given.

____

____

____

____

____

Unit II

LINGUISTIC MEDIATION

An *Overview of* Linguistic Mediation

UNIT II, OBJECTIVE 1
Demonstrate sound decision-making about when and how to provide linguistic mediation

Linguistic mediation refers to any act or utterance by the interpreter that briefly suspends the interpreted session or takes place outside the session and is intended to clarify linguistic barriers to communication.

Deciding when and how to clarify a linguistic barrier is a challenging task for all interpreters. The analytical and decision-making skills required are complex.

Unit II of this manual provides information on how to provide safe and effective linguistic mediation to address barriers to communication while adhering to ethical canons. Even trained interpreters find it challenging to perform linguistic mediation appropriately and with ease. Nearly all interpreters will benefit from thinking deeply about these issues, applying specific criteria to each situation and making decisions based on those criteria.

In order to perform successful linguistic mediation, the interpreter must first master the basic modes used in legal interpreting. Following an overview of modes, the interpreter will be introduced to guidelines for conducting a "pre-conference" with the attorney to help reduce linguistic barriers to communication that might arise during the session. (This curriculum strongly recommends that a pre-conference be conducted prior to every first encounter between a legal interpreter and a legal services provider.) The remainder of Unit II focuses on: basic linguistic mediation concepts and skills, with a particular emphasis on decision-making; the steps for linguistic mediation; and effective techniques and strategies for performing linguistic mediation.

Modes of Interpreting

The conventional understanding is that language operates mathematically, with each word in one language having an exact, corresponding word in another. This view presupposes that, even within a single language, each word, phrase, or sentence has a unitary meaning. By this account, interpretation is merely a process of decoding, or transliteration. In reality, language difference so deeply complicates the lawyering process because language and communication are contextual and often ambiguous processes.

—*Ahmad (2007:99)*

Review of Modes

Only three modes of interpreting are acceptable in legal settings:

- Consecutive
- Simultaneous (including whisper simultaneous)
- Sight translation

The mode that is not acceptable in any legal setting is summarization. Summarizing involves omitting portions of the message and changing the message. (Note that many interpreters do not even consider "summarization" or "summary" to be a mode of interpreting.) It should be emphasized that the interpreter is not trained or qualified to make decisions about which portions of the message, legal or otherwise, are important or unimportant and thus can be omitted.

The default mode in interview interpreting (attorney-client, prosecutor-witness, law enforcement-suspect for example) is consecutive. The bulk of the work of the legal interpreter outside the courtroom involves interview interpreting, where the interpreter should rely primarily on consecutive mode.

Consecutive Mode

The consecutive mode involves rendering a message from the source language into the target language after a pause in speech. Thus, consecutive interpreting involves a delay where the speaker suspends his/her statements to allow the interpreter to render the message. Consecutive interpreting is undertaken after a speaker has completed an utterance or thought.

Interpreting in consecutive mode constitutes the bulk of the interpreter's work with legal service providers. Some research suggests that consecutive is more accurate than simultaneous mode, perhaps because consecutive offers the interpreter the opportunity to capture and render the complete message. Once the interpreter has heard the entire message before interpreting it, the interpreter can make more accurate judgments about its meaning and a better choice of renditions.

Some interpreters consider consecutive mode a difficult skill and prefer to utilize simultaneous mode even during attorney-client interviews. However, consecutive mode supports accuracy and helps the interpreter to convey the message precisely to promote clear communication.

Most inexperienced interpreters find that they can accurately interpret one or two sentences in consecutive mode. While they should strive to enhance their memory skills, it is also important that they recognize their limits. They should not hesitate to interrupt speakers who go on too long, or to request repetitions as needed.

In addition, simultaneous is a very demanding skill that places more demands on the interpreter and requires such a high level of concentration that two interpreters are needed when the interpreted proceeding continues for a longer period of time.

Typically, however, only one interpreter is provided for legal interpreting outside the courtroom, and that is another reason consecutive mode is necessary.

Simultaneous mode

Interpreting in simultaneous mode involves rendering a message from a source language into a target language while the message is still being spoken, with a very brief lag time between source and target language utterances. The longer the lag (within reason), the more time the interpreter will have to absorb the meaning of the whole utterance and gain an idea where it is going. However, the length of the lag will depend at least in part on the memory skills of the interpreter. The longer the lag, in general, the more accurate the rendering is likely to be.

Simultaneous mode, which is often required in courtroom settings, is rarely used in attorney-client interviews or any setting that involves questions and answers. However, simultaneous interpreting may be used at times when real-time interpreting is required. For instance, when someone is excited or distressed and is speaking rapidly without pausing, it might be necessary to switch into simultaneous mode. Other cases could involve an emergency situation, an emotional situation where the interpreter does not wish to interrupt to request a pause, interpreting for children, or interpreting for someone who does not understand the need to pause (due, for example, to age, disability or illness).

In general, in legal interpreting it is preferred that simultaneous mode be used when the non-English speaker is only listening and is not expected to respond. (This mode is also used when the English speaker is listening to the interpreted statements by a non-English-speaker, *e.g.*, when a non-English speaker makes a victim impact statement to the court at sentencing.)

Simultaneous mode makes many demands on interpreters that can increase fatigue and erode accuracy (see *e.g.*, Vidal, 1997). For this reason, in legal settings such as courtrooms that require the use of simultaneous mode, it is strongly recommended that two interpreters be used. They can switch places roughly every 15 minutes or half an hour, depending on their fatigue level.

Whisper is a form of simultaneous mode. In whisper interpreting (also known as whispered simultaneous or *chuchotage*), the interpreter speaks to the recipient of the interpreted message in a low voice or by whispering. Whisper interpreting is often used in court and also for public information sessions, *e.g.*, during public talks about employment law or immigration services. If no specialized equipment is available to reduce the sound of the interpreter's voice, the interpreter speaks in a whisper or near-whisper while sitting or standing close to the person or group for whom he or she is interpreting. Traditionally this mode was often used when a public presenter who speaks English addresses a group that includes LEP participants.

However, simultaneous interpreting equipment is now commonly seen in community settings. Thus, these days, whisper simultaneous is rarely necessary because even nonprofit agencies, schools, health departments and libraries, as well as contract interpreters themselves, are purchasing or renting interpreting equipment. When using such equipment, the interpreter may be positioned at a distance from the individual or small group that needs the interpreter and speak in a low voice through a special microphone to the target-language speakers, who are equipped with special receivers to hear the interpreter. This is a discreet and effective way to provide simultaneous interpreting in public settings. It permits the interpreter to whisper into a transmitter to reduce the distraction of an interpreter speaking aloud. The LEP individuals do not even need to group themselves together but can choose to sit wherever they wish.

In legal services, whisper interpreting might be used for public sessions, *e.g.*, workshops, court hearings or programs about an agency's services if the number of LEP individuals is small enough. Simultaneous interpreting in general, with or without such equipment, should not be used, for client-attorney interviews except in situations of group representation. Some interpreters purchase their own simultaneous interpreting equipment, consisting of a portable transmitter pack for the interpreter and small receivers for the listener(s). However, even if they own such equipment, they should not bring it to interpreted sessions for legal services providers.

To summarize the points made above, outside the courtroom legal interpreters should switch to simultaneous only when:

■ Other individuals in the interview are speaking to each other and the client needs to listen to the discourse in real time.

■ A speaker becomes so excited that he or she will not pause. In this situation, continuing in consecutive mode will exceed the interpreter's memory.

■ An emergency occurs.

■ A speaker is confused (*e.g.*, due to mental illness, age, disability, dementia, or the understanding of a young child) and will not pause to let the interpreter interpret.

"When an individual is missing a word, it's not just a word. It's something that will make or break your case."

—*Estella Zamora, interpreter coordinator, Idaho*
—*Stewart (2008)*

Sight translation

Sight translation involves rendering a written text orally into the target language. Common examples of documents that might be sight translated include retainer agreements (contracts) between the client and the organization; complaints and motions filed with the court; affidavits; court orders; and application forms.

Steps for Successful Sight Translation

1. Make sure that the legal services provider remains in the room to answer questions. In addition to the fact that an attorney needs to be present to answer client questions, leaving the client alone with an interpreter can lead to a situation where information is disclosed that should not be discussed outside of the presence of the attorney. One possible consequence is to jeopardize attorney-client privilege.

2. Make sure the text does not exceed the interpreter's competence. Respectfully but firmly decline to sight translate long, complex documents with difficult terminology.

3. Read the whole text silently to be sure of understanding it.

4. Identify unfamiliar concepts and potential language barriers, such as complex sentence structures and unfamiliar terms. Either ask the attorney to clarify unfamiliar terminology or consult a dictionary or other resource.

5. Analyze the language register and language patterns.

6. Render the document into the target language sentence by sentence, with no additions, changes or deletions.

7. Maintain the same grammar, style and register as the source document.

When performing sight translation, the interpreter should always remember to read the text silently from beginning to end, to be sure of understanding it well, before performing the sight translation, even if there are time constraints. The interpreter should then render a *complete* oral translation of the document accurately and faithfully, without omitting, editing, adding to or explaining any part of it.

Under no circumstance should the interpreter summarize the text. If asked to do so, the interpreter should state that he or she is under an ethical obligation to render the entire document. The legal services provider may summarize the text, however, and the interpreter could interpret the provider's summary.

Sight translation is one of the most common tasks for interpreters in legal services. It is a challenging task, for many reasons:

1. The technical language, jargon and terminology in a legal text can be difficult even for experienced legal interpreters.

2. The high register, complex terminology and stilted syntax of many legal texts may be difficult to render spontaneously and accurately. Even certified legal translators often struggle with such texts.

3. Legal translation work usually involves a considerable amount of time. Sight translation is performed quickly on the spot.

4. If the interpreter renders a perfectly accurate sight translation, the client may still not understand what the document means.

5. The interpreter may not have had time to prepare and may lack access to reference materials to look up unfamiliar terms.

Legal interpreters should therefore examine the document first to see if it is too long or exceeds the technical knowledge and expertise of the interpreter. In some cases, the interpreter could request a break to look up complex terminology or request to take the document home if it is too long and there is insufficient time to look up new terms.

If possible, legal services providers should give the interpreters some of the documents to be sight translated in advance of the session, so that the interpreter has time to review them. Alternatively, the attorney could orally paraphrase the document.

However, if the text is too difficult and these options are not available, the interpreter can and must decline to sight translate it on ethical grounds. The ethical canons for declining to perform a sight translation include professionalism and accuracy as well as role boundaries and impediments to performance, if the interpreter is being asked to perform a task that goes beyond his or her training and/or qualifications.

Summary

Summarizing is not permitted in legal interpreting. It involves condensing a message and then rendering the condensed version into the target language. Thus this utterance becomes a creation of the interpreter, not the original speaker. Summarizing is highly prone to errors, filtering and significant changes by the interpreter. *Using the interpreter's personal judgment to alter the message in any way during an attorney-client interview or other legal proceeding is dangerous and could result in inaccurate communication between the attorney and his client.*

In summarizing, it is the interpreter who decides which elements in the message are important and which are unimportant. That should be the attorney's decision or the client's, not the interpreter's.

Why Summary is Not Permitted

When an interpreter is allowed to summarize, she is being permitted to decide or evaluate what portion of testimony or statements is relevant. An interpreter is not qualified to make such determinations.

—NAJIT (2005:1)

The Pre-Conference

Question: If the legal services provider asks the interpreter, before the interpreted session, "What can you tell me about the culture of this client?" how should the interpreter respond?

Answer: The interpreter should politely inform the attorney or provider that he or she is not an expert on cultural issues. She might suggest that the attorney may wish to consult the client directly to inquire about important cultural issues relevant to the case or consult with a cultural anthropologist or other cultural expert.

There are, broadly speaking, two types of linguistic mediation: mediation that takes place *during* the session (requiring the interpreter to interrupt the session) and mediation that takes place *outside* the session (such as a pre-conference). Each form of linguistic mediation carries a set of risks if the interpreter is unfamiliar with proper guidelines, professional techniques or limitations associated with the profession's scope of practice. In general, while interpreting, the interpreter should provide linguistic mediation only when necessary. By providing adequate information to the legal services provider *before* the session begins about how the interpreted session will proceed, the interpreter may be able to reduce the need for linguistic mediation.

What is a Pre-Conference? (Also known as a pre-session)

A pre-conference is a meeting held between the attorney and the interpreter before the interpreted session. A pre-conference may be particularly helpful if the attorney and interpreter have not worked together before, or if the case is new or complex. During the pre-conference, the interpreter and legal services provider can discuss parameters for the interpreted session. This meeting provides an opportunity for the attorney or provider to ask the interpreter questions about interpreting and for the interpreter to clarify her professional role.

What are the Differences Between a Pre-Conference and an Introduction?

An introduction is performed quickly at an initial meeting. A pre-conference is usually a sit-down discussion (though not always) and will be longer and more detailed than an introduction, with time for questions and answers on both sides.

The Need for a Pre-Conference

Many attorneys are unfamiliar with the role of the professional interpreter. A pre-conference may help to reduce the risk of an attorney engaging the interpreter in a side conversation during the session. During a pre-conference, the interpreter can make clear how the interpreted session will unfold. As needed, the interpreter may act as an expert on interpreting and on linguistic issues that can impede communication. Even then, the interpreter will have to be careful about his or her professional limitations and expertise.

Another reason for holding a pre-conference with the attorney is that the attorney is responsible for conducting the case in an ethical manner. The attorney is therefore liable if the interpreter acts inappropriately, in a way that harms the client's best interests.

Challenges That May Arise During a Pre-Conference

The interpreter must know how to respond to questions that may arise during a pre-conference. Common examples include questions from the attorney about cultural matters or questions pertaining to the client's state of mind, the client's beliefs or the interpreter's perception of a client's honesty. These are common and innocent questions. However, the interpreter lacks the knowledge and expertise needed to answer them. The interpreter is not a trained expert in these areas, nor can the interpreter read the client's mind.

If such questions arise during the interpreted session, they are awkward to answer because the interpreter is duty-bound to interpret everything that is said to both parties. A pre-conference with the attorney can prevent such misunderstandings.

How Long Will the Pre-Conference Last?

Depending on whether the attorney asks many questions or simply shares highlights about the case, a pre-conference could be as brief as two minutes or as long as 20 minutes or more. If the attorney has received specialized training about how to work with interpreters (which is highly recommended), the pre-conference could focus primarily on specific or sensitive aspects of the case and on any terminology that the interpreter might need to know.

How to Conduct a Pre-Conference

During a pre-conference, the interpreter could first make a professional introduction as outlined in Unit I followed by the following suggested components. The interpreter should select only those elements in the list on the next page that seem relevant and helpful.

- If the interpreter has a copy of the document "Working with Interpreters Outside of the Courtroom: A Guide for Legal Services Providers," prepared by Ayuda (**www.ayuda.com**), she may ask if the attorney has received it from the legal services agency. If not, the interpreter can offer a copy of that document.

- As needed, clarify the differences between interpreting (oral), translation (written) and sight translation (the oral translation of documents).

- Clearly outline the parameters and limitations of the interpreter's role. See the section on professional introductions in Unit I for details.

- Explain the appropriate use of first person. Emphasize that its use enhances accuracy and promotes direct communication between the lawyer and the client.

- Request that the lawyer speak directly to the client, not to the interpreter.

- State that *everything said during the interview* will be interpreted. Side conversations with the interpreter should not take place.

- Explain that legal interpreters are bound by a code of ethics. Offer the attorney a copy of the relevant code (use the code required by the interpreter in that local jurisdiction or the *Standards of Practice for Interpreters in Legal Services* included in Unit I of this manual).

- Request that, if possible, you be positioned beside and slightly behind the client unless, for any reason, the client is uncomfortable with that position. Mention that this position puts the attorney face to face with the client, leaves the interpreter in the background, makes it difficult for the client to look at/talk to the interpreter, and generally promotes a direct relationship and direct communication between the attorney and client. Suggest that the "triangle" position tends to create a situation where people are much more likely to look at, speak to and distract the interpreter, which may promote side conversations.

- State firmly that the interpreter is not an expert on the client's culture or psychology, but only on interpreting.

- If questions related to cultural expertise or the client's personal feelings or beliefs are asked, inform the attorney that the interpreter is not a cultural expert and cannot comment on the client's culture or state of mind but only on interpreting procedures and issues related to linguistic communication.

- Point out that in order to help promote confidentiality, ensure attorney-client privilege and support the attorney-client relationship, the interpreter and client should not be left alone together. (Attorneys may not be aware how common it is for clients to strike up detailed conversations with interpreters when left alone with them.) Therefore, if the attorney walks out of the room during the interview, the interpreter should also leave the room. If the client approaches the interpreter in the hallway or outside the room, the interpreter must direct the client to the attorney or his/her staff.

- Explain that it is customary for an interpreter to take notes to facilitate accurate interpreting, but that due to the sensitive nature of, and legal restrictions surrounding, attorney-client interviews, any notes regarding the session will be left with the attorney.

- Ask if there is any sensitive or technical information that the interpreter should know ahead of time and if the attorney will be using any specialized legal terms.

- State that the interpreter may perform sight translation of documents but is not a qualified translator and may not provide written translations of documents (unless, of course, the interpreter is a trained, professional and preferably certified translator).

- Ask if there are any documents to be sight translated that the interpreter can review prior to the interviews to help ensure a more accurate sight translation.

- Conclude by stating that sometimes clients leave the session without a full understanding, even when the interpreter interprets accurately. The only way for the attorney to be sure that the client has understood the session clearly is to request that the client repeat his or her understanding of the case and what the client must do next. Having an interpreter is no substitute for checking for understanding since it is common for clients to lack understanding of U.S. culture, the judicial system and the legal process. (While this may be true for many fully English-proficient residents, the problem is particularly common among LEP clients.)

- Ask the attorney if he/she has any questions prior to the interview.
- Answer any questions related to the upcoming interview.
- Politely decline to answer questions that exceed the scope of the interpreter's role or expertise and state why you cannot answer.

Note that a pre-conference is not necessary with the client. Instead, a professional introduction that lays down clear parameters for the interpreted session, as outlined in Unit I of this manual, should be held with the client so that the client understands how the session will proceed. During that introduction the interpreter may add any relevant points that appear to be appropriate and necessary.

Bilingual Staff

Bilingual employees who serve as interpreters should be professionally trained in legal interpreting and tested for language proficiency, like any other legal interpreter. While many people feel that bilingual staff in legal services should not be used to interpret, if appropriately trained and qualified to interpret, they do have many advantages in their work. They typically know the legal services providers well, including some of the communication issues that may arise, and are familiar with the terminology and subject matter of the interpreted session.

However, bilingual employees also face unique challenges, including: difficulty-setting boundaries with colleagues, difficulty in declining certain requests, and remembering not to perform their (other) job while interpreting. Bilingual staff members also face the same challenges as contract interpreters, including a lack of knowledge of the terminology in the target language (even if they are familiar with the terminology in English). Therefore,

bilingual staff should be provided with the same training as others working in the legal field. Bilingual staff should also adhere to the requirements of accuracy and the duty to withdraw from a case if it exceeds their expertise. It is also highly recommended that bilingual staff be tested for language proficiency in both the source and target language.

Bilingual staff may wish to conduct a presentation for their coworkers after completing this training. Unless other staff members have been trained to work with a professional interpreter, they may be confused about how interpreted sessions with the bilingual employee will now proceed. Points to emphasize include:

- Bilingual employees who interpret in legal settings must adhere to the same code of ethics and standards of practice that other legal interpreters follow.
- Providers should not speak to or ask questions of the interpreter as a colleague during the session. (Any consultations with the bilingual employee about a client must take place either before or after the session.)
- When bilingual employees interpret, they are not permitted to perform their other duties *while* interpreting. For example, a bilingual employee who also interprets could help a client fill out forms (if that is part the employee's job), but only before or after the appointment. During the session, he or she could interpret for the provider, who would ask the questions and fill out the form; however, the interpreter must not do so.
- Interpreters are not permitted to sign as witnesses during the session. They may however sign any documents as the *interpreter*, including documents for which they have performed sight translation.
- While serving as the interpreter, the bilingual employee should not be left alone with the client.
- Bilingual employees who are not qualified to perform translation should decline on ethical grounds due to the legal risk and liability.
- If a client asks, "Didn't you tell me last time this wouldn't happen?" the bilingual employee who interpreters should simply interpret the question—not answer it.

Note-Taking

Information given in this manual on note-taking and memory skills is for background information only. Improving these skills is not addressed in *The Language of Justice* training program.

Question:	Why do professional interpreters come prepared to take notes?
Answer:	Interpreters are human, and research shows that human memory is highly unreliable. In addition, it is not always possible to interrupt two speakers.

An interpreter is encouraged to interrupt the speakers when the information given exceeds the interpreter's memory retention. Short-term memory retention varies from individual to individual. While interpreters continuously strive to increase their memory retention, good note-taking skills assist the interpreter with memory retention.

Some interpreters develop excellent note-taking skills, and others may not. At a minimum, an interpreter should jot down names, places/addresses, dates and numbers but it may be necessary to write down much more. It is important for legal interpreters to develop their memory skills and also to come prepared to take notes. The more highly developed the interpreter's memory skills, the less need there will be for note taking.

The legal interpreter should arrive with strategies and plans for note taking. Here are a few things interpreters should be prepared to jot down to ensure accuracy:

1. **Numbers.** Community and even court interpreters often fail to accurately render numbers without taking notes (Mazza, 2001).
2. **Technical terms**, especially unfamiliar ones.
3. **Acronyms.**
4. **Lists.** After three or four items, lists become difficult to remember.
5. **Unusual or idiomatic expressions.** Some expressions are a challenge both to remember and to interpret.
6. **Steps.** Information rendered in the form of steps to be taken by a client may be difficult for the interpreter to memorize in the correct order.
7. **Instructions.** Instructions are similar to steps, and must be accurately interpreted. If a client fails to follow up on instructions, this could jeopardize the legal outcome.
8. **Proper nouns.** Names and places are often hard to understand and difficult to remember.
9. **Legal jargon.** Legal terms may tax the interpreter's memory, particularly if they cluster together.

The interpreter must exercise judgment. Not all of the items noted in this list need to be preserved in notes on every occasion. They are items that have been noted by experts in the field as those that are particularly difficult to remember without note-taking.

Key Elements of a Message

Some of the important elements to jot down in interpreter notes may include:

- Essential ideas. Experienced note-takers can capture a whole idea with a symbol.
- First and last sentences. These often contain important information.
- Links. The relationship between different parts of an utterance (like next steps) can be confusing if they are interpreted out of order.
- Causality. If one thing causes the next, this connection must be clear in the interpreter's mind and notes.
- Transcodable terms. Some words should not be interpreted but simply rendered "as is" into the other language (*e.g.*, certain legal charges with no conceptual equivalence in the target language). These may be referred to as "transcodable" terms and followed by a paraphrase, a request for clarification or a linguistic mediation (see Module B below). Possible examples: *Temporary Protected Status (TPS), constructive termination, and protection order.*

A Word About Shorthand

Interpreters often mention shorthand and think that note taking should be a form of shorthand. This is incorrect. Shorthand is a symbolic writing method intended to record whole conversations. It was used extensively by secretaries and administrative assistants taking dictation. If an interpreter tries to record a whole conversation, he or she will be unable to interpret. It is both impossible and dangerous to take shorthand while interpreting.

The interpreter should not be taking detailed notes, but rather only noting down those elements that might be difficult to recapture or recall accurately.

Symbols

Symbols have many advantages in note taking. For example, they are visual and compact. They can express many ideas in little space, and they take less time to write down than complete words.

In addition, symbols are not language. This helps to avoid the confusion that often occurs in note taking between the interpreter's two working languages. (The interpreter may take notes in Spanish when the individual was speaking English, for example, or vice versa.)

Each interpreter should develop his or her own set of symbols. This is a wise and necessary strategy, but the interpreter should do this ahead of time. Although each interpreter will tend to have a personal system, it can be dangerous to improvise symbol systems on the spot (as the interpreter may incorrectly remember what the symbol means and make an important error).

A few remarks on symbols. First, they should be simple and clear. Use them for:

- Common concepts (e.g., landlord-tenant terms, standard legal forms).
- Technical terms that recur frequently.
- Ideas or instructions common to that legal services provider (e.g., the requirements needed to initiate a civil protective order).

Common symbols used by interpreters can include such symbols as the ones below (with any meaning the interpreter wants to assign to a given symbol):

1. Arrows. Arrows can be used to indicate direction but they may also show an INCREASE (arrow goes up) or a DECREASE (arrow goes down): ↔ ← ↑ → ↓ ↵
2. Basic math symbols: >, <, =, ⁓, ± (can be used with their usual meaning)
3. Science/mathematical symbols: ∑, °, ϒ, Ψ, Ω, ς, α, Θ, Ξ, ∴, ∏
4. Symbols in common usage: √, φ, ♣, ♦, ♥, ♠, *, ◻, ○, ♂
5. Shapes (squares, circles, trapezoids, triangles, etc.).
6. Punctuation marks: ? ! ( ) " :
7. Instant message style notations: 4U, IC
8. Keyboard symbols: *, &, ^, %, $, #, @

Abbreviations and Shortcuts

Abbreviations are common in legal services. The interpreter should develop an additional list of those abbreviations that recur often in a particular service where the interpreter often interprets. For example, in immigration services the term "application for naturalization" (application for citizenship) could be noted down by the interpreter as "N-400", which is the name and number of the form. This is an easy abbreviation for interpreters in immigration services to remember. An interpreter who interprets for special education legal cases might use SLAR for "speech/language assessment results for reevaluation." In family law, PO could stand for a protection order.

In addition, the interpreter should keep a list of legal terms or phrases that recur often and could be abbreviated. A small-coiled handbook with a hardy cover is often ideal for this purpose.

Margins

Another common note-taking skill of professional interpreters involves the use of margins. Margins do not have to be literal; if desired, the interpreter can simply leave some blank space on the left side of the page. What is important is whatever the interpreter decides to write in the margins.

The goal of margin notes is to help the interpreter to mentally organize the information on the right side of the margin in a way that makes it easier to remember. For example, if there is a series of instructions, steps or facts being given to a client, the interpreter could write in the left hand margin:

1.
2.
3.

The numbers would indicate the steps. Symbols to help remember the steps could be noted beside each number. Other points that interpreters note in margins may include:

- Numbers, dates
- Contrasts, *e.g.*, before and after (a court filing, a hearing, a deadline)
- Comparisons, *e.g.*, citizen child; sibling; undocumented parent
- Categories (such as directions, types of proceedings)
- Requirements (*e.g.*, documents to submit)
- Key terms or information

Diagrams

For visual learners in particular, note taking in the form of diagrams, outlines, graphs, drawings, etc. may be helpful.

For example, if someone is telling a story about a personal experience that involved going from place to place, a simple map marking the places (perhaps noted in abbreviations) with arrows to indicate the order might be helpful.

Common Mistakes in Note-Taking

Interpreters who are new to note-taking often fall into the following common traps:

- They fail to prepare a note-taking system ahead of time.
- They forget to bring paper and pens.
- They write notes that are far too detailed.
- While writing many notes, they fail to listen and get lost.
- They confuse two working languages in their notes.
- They write notes literally, instead of using symbols and shortcuts.
- They use unclear symbols.
- They get behind in interpreting because they glance back at their notes and then miss important details in what is said.

Another danger (and it is surprisingly easy to do) is to take notes without thinking about them. One

can indeed take notes automatically, but notes taken in this way are likely to be less accurate and less easy to reconstitute into a message than notes taken with the interpreter's full awareness.

It is vital to pay close attention while note taking and process the information taken in the notes. Such notes should target the *meaning* of the message, not only the mechanical details.

Memory Skills
Memory load

Generally, interpreters who are starting out find that they can accurately recall only one or two sentences of spoken utterances. In order to interpret accurately, they will typically need to interrupt the speaker after one or two sentences.

Interpreters should not hesitate to interrupt at any time they feel the need to do so, because the main goal is accuracy and completeness, not memory retention. Good memory retention can take time to develop and varies from interpreter to interpreter.

While good short-term memory is an essential cognitive ability that interpreters must possess, their recall capabilities vary widely.

Interpreters therefore strive to increase memory retention. This can take years of practice, enhancement of one's note-taking skills and familiarity with the subject matter. The more familiar the interpreter becomes with the subject matter, the easier it becomes to retain longer passages.

Some experts therefore believe that short-term memory skills are among the first skills that all interpreters should be taught.

Short-term and long-term memory

Factors that can interfere with the interpreter's concentration include background noises, such as crying babies or pneumatic drills. Other distractions can include nervousness, visible emotional distress in the client, anger or dramatic personal stories (such as asylees who recount their experiences of war and torture). Almost any potent distraction can interfere with the interpreter's ability to retain information effectively.

In addition, if the interpreter has personally experienced the type of difficult situation recounted by a client, (*e.g.*, sexual assault, domestic violence, or a messy and painful divorce) this can also interfere with concentration. In extreme cases, the interpreter might need to withdraw, or decline the session ahead of time. Even in ideal circumstances, short-term memory is limited. In general, most people run into trouble when trying to remember more than about seven chunks of information.

Building memory skills

Every interpreter has a unique way to enhance memory skills. The important point is to work on it and develop the system that works for the interpreter.

Memory skills build on careful listening and attentive processing. One way to approach memory skills development is to divide it into the following steps for practice:

1. Active listening
2. Message scanning (for units of meaning)
3. Note-taking
4. Message analysis/decoding
5. Reconstructing the message

1. Active listening involves more than paying attention. The interpreter must be focused and ready to take apart the utterances and analyze them. This involves the ability to exclude outside distractions, to forget oneself and to become utterly absorbed in the message.

2. Message scanning means parsing every utterance for smaller units that hold meaning. The units of *meaning* (rather than words) will be mentally processed by the interpreter and perhaps written down in the interpreter's notes, as needed. For example, *lui tirer les vers du nez* in French will not be processed or remembered by the interpreter as "drawing worms out of his nose" but (depending on context) something more like, "getting him to cough up the information."

3. Note-taking: At every stage the interpreter will have to make an on-the-spot decision about whether a particular point (such as a number, date, time, place or person) might be easy to forget and should therefore be written down in notes.

4. Message analysis/decoding: This is a critical process that is most often unconscious. But the interpreter must make that process conscious through a deliberate effort to capture the meaning of the entire utterance.

5. Reconstructing the message: Once the meaning is clear and the different parts or the utterance analyzed, the interpreter must swiftly re-encode the meaning into the appropriate words in the target language.

Effective Strategies

What works? There are a number of helpful strategies to improve memory skills.

- Shadowing exercises: repeat at the same time, word for word ("parrot-style") in the same language, following a taped segment or a live speaker's words for the equivalent of several paragraphs of speech. This exercise is especially recommended for increasing skills in simultaneous mode.

- Engage in practice of both consecutive and simultaneous mode with professional interpreter tapes (such as those listed in the resources section of this manual).

- Have a friend tape texts of about 20 to 40 words each, then play the tape, listen and try to interpret the whole text—without taking notes.

- Conduct practice with some active interference, including loud background noise like music.

- Television or radio practice: perform consecutive or simultaneous interpreting, out loud or mentally, while listening to television or radio.

- Practice, practice, practice!

Each interpreter will develop individual techniques to enhance memory during a session. For example, some interpreters when hearing a series of steps will count the steps on their fingers and/or visualize each step. Some create and follow a story-line in their head. What works well for one interpreter may be different for another. Each interpreter, like each encounter, is unique.

For consecutive practice, try taping a television program such as a case on court TV. Then play back a short segment, hit the pause button and interpret. To make this a meaningful learning experience, be sure to tape your own performance. Now play back the first sentence or two of the original and then the first sentence or two of your own interpreted version to verify any aspects of the grammar or vocabulary that need strengthening. It may also help to make a list of the terms that were difficult.

Introduction to Linguistic Mediation

Clarifying a linguistic confusion is a vital task for all interpreters.

Linguistic mediation refers to any act or utterance by the interpreter that briefly suspends the interpreted session or takes place outside the session and is intended to clarify linguistic barriers to communication.

In legal services, as in other areas of interpreting, when interpreters perform linguistic mediation, they must consciously make every effort to do so *appropriately, professionally and without engaging in a side conversation or interfering with the attorney-client relationship.* At no point may the interpreter become an active participant in the encounter; he or she may speak as the interpreter only to address a linguistic barrier to communication. (Note that this rule is much stricter than the guidelines on how to perform mediation in community interpreting.)

The parameters for an interpreter's active role in legal settings are well defined. Interpreters may not converse with either party while interpreting. If the interpreter suspends the session, she must be brief. The interpreter should speak to the attorney first, then the client, and interpret to the client everything that is said to both parties.

Personal involvement by the interpreter is not permitted because allowing it (for example, by permitting a legal interpreter to offer explanations or opinions about the cultural nature of a communication) could result in an adverse effect on the client, the attorney or the case. It could also expose the interpreter to legal liability or damage his or her reputation. (One interpreter who held conversations with and picked up faxes for an imprisoned defendant was later imprisoned for conspiracy.)

In general, the interpreter's scope of practice in legal settings is strictly limited as discussed below. The restrictions laid out in Unit II will not harm the client, the quality of communication or the interview. On the contrary, these restrictions protect the client's access to justice and the attorney's ability to perform competently and effectively. They also protect the interpreter from liability.

Many trained interpreters perform linguistic mediation. They may call it "mediation," "intervening" or "clarification." However, it should be noted that the rules and guidelines in this manual conform to the *profession of legal interpreting.* Those rules, therefore, differ in both scope and content from those discussed in programs that address mediation or intervening in other areas of interpreting.

Examples of interpreter training programs that speak of "intervening" "mediation," or "clarification," include:

Bridging the Gap (Cross-Cultural Health Care Program), The Community Interpreter (Cross-Cultural Communications), various programs by AHECs (Area Health Education Centers), The Bilingual Medical Assistant (Phoenix Children's Hospital) and The Essential Piece (Culturesmart)

When to Provide Linguistic Mediation
General Criteria for Deciding When Linguistic Mediation is Appropriate

Principles

Deciding when and how to provide linguistic mediation is an important question. In the legal interpreting field, there is a general consensus on the following principles. They help the interpreter decide if, when and how to interrupt the interpreted session:

1. The interpreter should provide linguistic mediation only to support accurate, faithful interpreting.

2. When linguistic mediation is needed, the interpreter should provide it *briefly*

(for example, to request clarification or repetition) and then continue interpreting.

3. While performing linguistic mediation, the interpreter should not engage in side conversations with the attorney or the client.

4. The interpreter should make her comments in both languages and interpret all response(s).

5. The interpreter may provide linguistic mediation when communication begins to break down due to culture-related terminology but should exercise great caution when doing so.

6. The interpreter should not provide cultural expertise except to clarify culturally bound terms expressing concepts relevant to the interview.

7. Providing linguistic mediation must not include the interpreter's impression of a client's state of mind, dishonesty or truthfulness. Only the attorney can make those determinations.

8. The interpreter should not advocate for the client. Only the attorney may advocate for the client.

Outside the session the following guidelines are applicable:

1. The legal interpreter should not conduct linguistic mediation with **clients** outside a session. Doing so could jeopardize attorney-client privilege, and the client might divulge information that should be discussed only in the presence of the attorney. Moreover, the interpreter may be tempted to give advice. Any of these circumstances could put a case at risk.

2. If a client asks to speak with the interpreter or makes a request of the interpreter to provide clarification (which is common) the interpreter should politely state that she is not permitted to speak with the client unless the attorney is present and that she is not qualified to give the client information or advice, whether on legal or general subjects. The interpreter should then refer the client back to the attorney or the appropriate legal staff

and offer to interpret the client's question for the attorney. However, it is important that the interpreter inform the attorney of any such request or question that comes from the client outside of the attorney's presence. This allows the attorney to be completely aware of the client's needs and concerns at all time.

3. If the attorney wishes to speak to the interpreter outside the session, the interpreter may be consulted as an expert on *interpreting procedures, protocol and possible linguistic barriers to communication.* The interpreter must restrict his or her remarks to that scope of expertise.

4. The interpreter may provide insight into the nature of common linguistic barriers to communication that are influenced by culture *if such barriers are clear and commonly known.* For example, the confusion caused by the use of Spanish surnames often leads to miscommunications and is a problem widely known among Spanish interpreters that most of them are competent to clarify. However, attitudes toward women vary widely among all national groups and individuals; no interpreter of any language should make comments regarding the attitude of men toward women in a given culture.

5. Interpreters should avoid making broad cultural pronouncements, *e.g.*, "Women from that country never make a decision without their husband present." If the attorney asks, "Why does this client never seem to make a decision? Is there something cultural going on here that I should know about?" the interpreter should refrain from commenting about the client's state of mind because the interpreter cannot be in the mind of another person. Instead, s/he could state that there are many different attitudes toward decision-making in the culture of the client. The client may be the best person to provide informed input, and the attorney may wish to make inquiries of the client. (Any cultural issues about decision-making that come from the client will at least reflect the client's understanding, which will help the attorney better understand the client and perhaps other aspects of the case.)

6. Even when asked by the attorney for an opinion, the interpreter should refrain from giving an opinion. Ethical requirements prohibit the interpreter from offering or providing an opinion. Moreover, if the interpreter is mistaken (and opinions are, by definition, subjective), the interpreter's comments could lead the attorney and the case in a direction that is not helpful to the client. Both attorney and interpreter could be held jointly liable for any negative outcome that resulted from the interpreter's opinion.

7. The interpreter who avoids statements that are broadly subjective or personal helps to protect the client, the case, the attorney, the interpreter and the legal process.

Specific Circumstances When Linguistic Mediation is Appropriate

Providing linguistic mediation during the session

Linguistic mediation occurs whenever an interpreted session is briefly suspended by the interpreter to address a linguistic barrier to communication.

"Linguistic" mediation may involve an act as simple as requesting clarification of a term that the interpreter does not know or asking the attorney to turn down the air conditioner so that the interpreter can hear better. Linguistic mediation can also be more complex, for instance, when the interpreter steps in to clear up the confusion regarding a client's identity or paperwork by giving a brief explanation of relevant naming conventions among Amharic speakers.

For court interpreters, situations that fall into the category of simple linguistic mediation may feel like second nature. Court interpreters typically do not perceive what they are doing as "linguistic" mediation because, to them, it is simply part and parcel of their customary performance requirements under their Code of Professional Responsibility (for example, Canon 1, Accuracy and Completeness, or Canon 8 of the Code of Professional Responsibility: Assessing and Reporting Impediments to Performance).

However, even in simple cases, once the interpreter interrupts the session she is no longer interpreting. Doing so amplifies the risk of a side conversation, particularly in the less formal environment outside a courtroom. In general, providing linguistic mediation can be a simple or complex act, but it always carries risks. The risk is not only a side conversation. During a linguistic mediation, the interpreter might give inaccurate information to either party, offer advice or opinions, or otherwise violate the ethics and standards of the legal interpreting profession in a way that may jeopardize a case.

That said, in certain cases legal interpreters are not only permitted but required to provide linguistic mediation. For example, when interpreters need assistance to interpret accurately because they do not understand a term or cannot hear a speaker clearly, they *must* request clarification of that term.

The following criteria will help the interpreter decide when it is appropriate to provide linguistic mediation.

Auditory barriers to understanding

- **Loud noises or soft voices.** If any speaker is not clearly audible, request that the conditions be corrected (*e.g.*, ask to move to a different part of the room, request the individual to speak more loudly or ask that air conditioning be turned off).

- **Inaudible or unintelligible speech.** If a portion of speech is unclear, request a repetition.

- **Rapid speech/too few pauses.** If an individual is speaking too quickly, or failing to pause, request that the person slow down their speech and pause when asked.

- **Persistent interruptions/distractions/multiple voices.** Politely request that only one person speak at a time. If the problem continues, explain that the interpreter is obligated to interpret everything but cannot do so when more than one person speaks at the same time.

Clarification

- **Unclear/ambiguous use of language.** If a word, phrase or statement is ambiguous or unclear to the interpreter, request clarification. For example, *nipote* in Italian could mean niece/nephew or grandchild, and the context might not make the distinction clear. Similarly, *belle-mère* in French means either mother-in-law or stepmother. (Linguistic confusion caused by varying terms for family relations is common in many languages.)

- **Unfamiliar vocabulary/ idioms/regionalisms.** If the client or attorney uses vocabulary, idioms or regionalisms that the interpreter does not understand, the interpreter must request a clarification.

- **Unfamiliar legal terminology.** If the attorney uses an unfamiliar legal terminology (*e.g., parolee* in immigration law), request an explanation from the attorney and/or request permission to consult a bilingual legal dictionary, glossary or other resource for the exact translation of that term.

- **Lack of linguistic/conceptual equivalent.** If a word, phrase or statement used by the attorney or the client has no exact equivalent in the target language, inform the attorney to allow the attorney, client and interpreter to discuss an alternate solution to convey the information. *e.g.,* the concept of *comadre/compadre* in Spanish is complex, and might have relevance to the case. Instead of trying to explain it, the interpreter would provide linguistic mediation to inform the attorney that no exact equivalent of this term exists in English, giving the attorney an opportunity to discuss the term with the client.

- **Errors by the interpreter.** If the interpreter makes an error, correct it as soon as possible.

Competence

- **Scope of competence.** If the assignment exceeds the scope of the interpreter's competence, inform the attorney and request permission to withdraw from the session.

Barriers to understanding

- **Register.** If a legal term is used, and the interpreter senses that the client does not understand it because the register is too high, the interpreter *may not lower the register* or explain the term. Instead, interpret the term accurately, using the same register. If the interpreter sees that there is a communication breakdown due to the attorney's persistent use of highly technical language or high register, the interpreter should inform the attorney of the communication breakdown.

- **Client's lack of understanding.** It is not the legal interpreter's role to check for understanding. In extreme cases, the interpreter may intervene to state to all present that, "The interpreter senses a break in communication" (but must leave the attorney to address it). Sometimes, at the end of the session, particularly if the attorney does not follow recommended guidelines to check for the client understanding, the interpreter may have the strong impression that the client does not understand what the attorney said. If so, outside the session the interpreter could discuss with the attorney the importance of checking for understanding. If the problem persists, or is common at a particular legal services agency, the interpreter may (without revealing any details of a session) inform the interpreting service supervisor about the problem. Check with the interpreter service policy first. However, the interpreter should not reveal any details or opinions like, "The client had no idea what the attorney was talking about," or "The attorney told her she had a weak case but she thought that meant she would get a green card."

Culturally bound terms

- **General cultural references.** If there is no direct equivalent of a source language term in the target language, clarify the term, *e.g.,* a date that would have no meaning in English (whether because it is a religious holiday, because dates are expressed in a different order that may lead to a misunderstanding, or for another cultural reason). For example, the Chinese New Year does not take place on January 1, and its date varies according to the Chinese lunar calendar (falling anywhere between December and March on the Gregorian calendar used in the U.S.). Thus, if a Chinese client reports that something took place at New Year's, and the attorney becomes confused about dates, the interpreter may have to provide linguistic mediation to clarify the difference in dates between the two celebrations of the New Year.

- ***Specific cultural terms.*** If a term has cultural meaning that an English equivalent cannot convey, explain the term to the attorney. For example, the Spanish word *litargio* has no exact equivalent in English. The interpreter may have to clarify that *litargio* is a traditional powdered remedy sold in some herbal medicine shops. (Its legal relevance may be related to the fact that it contains up to 79 percent lead, which can cause irreversible brain damage.) Anytime an interpreter explains a culturally bound term, she should request that the attorney verify the interpreter's explanation with the client to ensure that the client has the same understanding of the term. At no time however, should the interpreter explain a legal term to the client. Explanation of legal terms should always be left to the attorney, as that is a critical element of the practice of law (if performed by the interpreter it could constitute the unauthorized practice of law).

- ***Complex cultural concepts.*** If a term has cultural meaning that is too complex to convey, **do not try to explain it.** Instead, state the problem clearly (*e.g., "The client has used a religious term,* **shahadah***, that I cannot adequately interpret into English"*) and allow the attorney to ask questions of the client. In the example just given, the word *shahadah* in Arabic refers to a statement of faith that constitutes one of the five pillars of Islam. (The *shahadah* refers a statement that means: *I testify that there is no God but God, and Muhammad is the Messenger of God.*) This term is filled with rich historical, cultural, emotional and religious resonance going back many centuries. It cannot be conveyed or adequately addressed by the interpreter during the session. If the term is relevant to the service being provided, it is preferable that the client, not the interpreter, should elaborate on its meaning. Otherwise, if the interpreter is Muslim, he or she could speak to the attorney during a pre-conference regarding **basic** facts concerning Islam that any practicing Muslim would know, for example, that the fasting month of Ramadan (a lunar month that varies according to the Islamic calendar) takes place at a different time each year. The interpreter could also briefly mention the difference between the Islamic and U.S. calendar, if this is relevant. For any information on Islam that is more complex, the attorney would need to consult an expert on Islam.

Other cultural barriers

The interpreter is broadly authorized to clarify common cultural-linguistic issues related to specific terms, using due discretion. The interpreter should always, in such situations, apply the broad criterion of whether the information provided is *simple and commonly known to interpreters of that language* and whether clarifying it is *necessary to ensure **accurate** communication.* Examples include:

- ***Names.*** The usage of names in many languages is a culturally-bound practice. For example, for Ethiopian clients, official documents for one individual may commonly have different last names, because of differences between the traditional Ethiopian naming system and the western naming system. In China and some other Asian countries, surnames and first names may be reversed. However, after the clients arrive in the U.S. their legal documents may follow the American naming system. Spanish-speaking clients may have some documents that show their father's last name and others that show the father and mother's last names.

- ***Titles.*** Titles may not be meant literally. For example, it may be a common practice for many in Egypt and Syria to address a respected person as *ustadh*, meaning "professor," regardless of the person's academic or professional background. The interpreter might use "sir" in English if appropriate, but if a client in legal proceedings uses a title uncommon in English, the interpreter might wish to alert the attorney to its true meaning in case the attorney has anything to suggest to the client about the use of titles in court settings.

- ***Spelling.*** Due to illiteracy, a common issue, clients may be unable to correctly spell their own name when requested. This problem can lead to legal confusion and contradictory spellings on various legal documents. Additionally, for languages that do not use the Roman alphabet, transliteration into English can be complex and lead to multiple spellings. (This problem has also led to some agencies' accidental creation of several files for the same client.)

- ***Dates, including birthdates***. In many countries, it may be common not to be certain of one's own birth date or for a person to be considered as being one year old on his or her date of birth. Dates may also be expressed in a different order than in the U.S.: for example, many countries use Day, Month, Year (4 May 2008 or 04/05/08) as opposed to the U.S. convention of Month, Day, Year (May 4, 2008 or 05/04/08). Birth certificates and other documents may reflect the alternative order. This point should be raised only if it is relevant and/or the different dating procedures are likely to cause problems for the case. Additionally, clients from countries or cultures that use a calendar other than the Gregorian calendar may have difficulty in converting dates accurately.

- Other examples of information that the interpreter is permitted to clarify in some circumstances include ***units of measurement, addresses, kinship terms, holidays, common ceremonies,*** etc. The interpreter may provide general information during or outside the interpreted session on such issues, always again applying the criterion of whether this information is commonly and widely known to interpreters of that language and relevant to the interpreted session. The interpreter should provide only objective, factual and relevant information.

Steps for Decision-Making in Linguistic Mediation

Outside the session, the interpreter should never conduct private conversations with the client and should provide linguistic mediation with the attorney only on request. During the interpreted session, decision-making is more complex. The interpreter must constantly assess the situation to monitor whether a barrier to understanding meets any of the criteria listed above for linguistic mediation. The following decision-making steps apply:

1. Assess and monitor the situation.

2. If a barrier to understanding arises, identify a criterion that triggers the need to provide linguistic mediation.

3. Make a decision about whether linguistic mediation is necessary, or whether accurate interpreting can take place without linguistic mediation.

4. If linguistic mediation is necessary, formulate an appropriate strategy.

5. Perform the mediation (*e.g.*, a correction, clarification or request for repetition). Keep it brief and interpret it into the other language.

6. Continue interpreting.

REMEMBER. The interpreter who does not know the meaning of a term or utterance must suspend the session to request clarification or consult a dictionary.

Steps for conducting linguistic mediation are discussed in the next chapter.

<table>
<tr><td>

The Importance of Appropriate Linguistic Mediation

Attorneys often raise their concern about interpreters who interject too much or too often. This legitimate concern stems from the fact that one of the key activities that attorneys engage in during attorney-client interviews is to make judgments about the credibility of the client. These judgment calls affect the strength of the case and the client's ability to perform well in a deposition or hearing. The more an interpreter interferes, the more difficult it becomes for the attorney to make that assessment accurately.

</td></tr>
</table>

Risks of Providing Linguistic Mediation *During* the Session

In legal interpreting, the consequences of side conversations may affect the case, jeopardize attorney-client privilege and/or inadvertently lead the interpreter to practice law without a license.

Everything spoken by any of the individuals, even a simple request by the interpreter for clarification of a term, must be interpreted. Side conversations, as innocent as they might be, could also have a negative effect on the attorney-client relationship. For example, a side conversation with the client could enhance the risk that the interpreter will unwittingly express opinions, mention personal feelings or give advice. On the other hand, a side conversation with the attorney could arouse the client's fear or suspicion about what is really taking place. It might erode the client's trust in the interpreter and interfere with the attorney's ability to build trust with the client.

Interpreters who carry the community interpreting practices of advocacy or cultural mediation (culture brokering) into legal settings risk violating ethics of legal interpreting. The consequences could be serious. For example, if the interpreter is court certified, and the violation is reported, the interpreter could be subject to disciplinary procedures and ultimately could have certification revoked. Even if the interpreter is not court certified, the case and the interpreter's reputation may be jeopardized.

Some of the risks inherent in improper linguistic mediation may also come from the actions of legal service providers who are not trained or accustomed to working with interpreters and may make requests that would violate the interpreter's ethical requirements. Examples of such requests are discussed in Unit III.

Another risk of linguistic mediation during the session is that the interpreters may offer a personal opinion about a cultural issue. The interpreter may provide only *general* information that is commonly known by linguistic (not cultural) experts in the field. The attorney is ultimately responsible and may be held liable for making certain that any culture-related information obtained from a non-expert is verified for its accuracy.

Risks of Providing Linguistic Mediation *Outside* the Session

Linguistic mediation outside the session may be provided only to the **attorney**, on request. As stated previously, once the interpreter opens the door to speaking with the client in the absence of the attorney, attorney-client privilege could be placed at risk. The client may also make statements to the interpreter that may not be in the best interest of the client.

However, problems may also arise when interpreters provide linguistic mediation with an attorney or legal services provider outside the session. The interpreter and attorney are encouraged to hold a pre-conference prior to the attorney-client interview. When legal services staff consult an interpreter after the session, the interpreter may be expected or asked to play a different role. For example, the interpreter may be expected to resolve problems, provide opinions about a client, investigate certain matters or even make purchases or deliveries. Such requests lie outside the interpreter's scope of practice and highlight the need to train legal services providers on how to work with interpreters. In the meantime, the interpreter must make a conscious effort to distinguish between appropriate and inappropriate requests (discussed in Unit III).

Sometimes, lawyers exert pressure on interpreters to perform acts that go beyond the scope of an interpreter. The pressure is usually well intentioned or unintentional because the attorney is not familiar with best practices of working with interpreters. In some instances, the attorney may have worked with untrained interpreters or bilingual advocates in the past, and these untrained interpreters might have performed such services because they did not know that doing so was inappropriate. This is particularly true in the case of bilingual advocates or bilingual staff members who have a dual role that may include support services.

As a result, the attorney might be under the impression that interpreters can, and should, perform such services as accompany the client to obtain a protection order without a legal services provider. In such situations, it is important to calmly and professionally explain the role of the interpreter.

Steps *for* Linguistic Mediation

The Steps for Linguistic Mediation

A review of basic steps for linguistic mediation

1. Interpret the last thing that was said by either party before beginning to provide linguistic mediation (unless you do not understand the utterance).
2. Suspend the session. Interrupt with a gesture and speak up.
3. Address the attorney first.
4. Inform both the attorney and the client what you are about to do (transparency).
5. Refer to yourself as the interpreter. (*"The interpreter would like to request the attorney to clarify a term."*)
6. Provide the same linguistic mediation with both the attorney and the client. (To attorney: *"The interpreter would like to request that you clarify the meaning of the term* **pro tem.** *"* To client: *"The interpreter has requested that the attorney clarify the meaning of the term* **pro tem.** *"*
7. **Keep the linguistic mediation brief and to the point.**
8. As soon as the client or attorney begins to speak, return to the role of interpreter and interpret that response.
9. **Continue interpreting.**

The Attorney's Stake in Linguistic Mediation

The attorney may be negatively affected by the interpreter's performance in a number of ways.

For example, if the case is lost, the client can file an ineffective assistance of counsel claim, and the attorney may be held responsible for inaccurate interpretation or the inappropriate conduct of the interpreter.

Why the interpreter must address the attorney first

When performing linguistic mediation, the interpreter addresses the attorney first because the attorney is legally responsible for the interpreter's conduct. The interpreter must notify the attorney before engaging in linguistic mediation (or any activity other than interpreting) so that the attorney may approve.

In some cases, if the interpreter requests a clarification the attorney may change his or her statements. In addition, if the interpreter addresses the client first, it may raise a red flag in the attorney's mind that the interpreter is engaging in a side conversation, thereby eroding the attorney's trust in the interpreter.

Transparency

Transparency means that all persons present know what the interpreter is discussing with any individual or group at all times. Before providing linguistic mediation with one person or group, always inform the lawyer and then the client what the interpreter is doing.

Failing to observe transparency violates the ethical canon of accuracy and completeness, which could affect the attorney-client relationship. A side conversation with the legal services provider may also make the client feel distrustful, concerned or confused.

Limitations on Role

The interpreter should make clear to the lawyer, if there is an opportunity to do so, that ***even when acting outside the session as a linguistic expert*** the interpreter has limitations on her role. For example, even outside the interpreted session:

- The interpreter must never *personalize* information, *e.g.*, if the attorney asks, "Why won't my client talk to me about her case?" the interpreter cannot say, "Because in her country no one talks about sexual assault." Instead she can say something like, "Sexual assault is still a difficult topic to discuss in [such-and-such a country or region]. So for many women from that area it may be difficult to discuss sexual assault for a legal case. But I cannot tell you if that is the case for this particular client. You may wish to explore that with your client."

- The interpreter may not *over generalize*. For example, if the attorney asks the interpreter why the client won't make a decision, the interpreter must not say, "Women from Mexico never make a decision without their husband or partner there." Instead she may say, "I really do not know. Sometimes it is difficult to get an answer on a legal decision if a woman's partner is not present, but this type of situation varies tremendously and may depend on the woman's education, family and her degree of independence. You might wish to ask her how she feels about making decisions on her own."

- The interpreter must avoid *stereotyping*. For example, if the lawyer wants to know whether the client is lying, the interpreter must never say something like, "Yes, I think your client is lying" or "People from this country can't be trusted." Instead, the interpreter could say, "I am sorry, but I really do not know whether your client is telling the truth or lying and it would be unethical for me to give you my personal opinion."

A True Story

Attorney: Is my client from Puerto Rico?

Interpreter: No.

> The interpreter was incorrect. The error had an impact on the outcome of the case.

Techniques *and* Strategies *for* Linguistic Mediation

Cultural Mediation and Advocacy

Why legal interpreters may not perform cultural mediation or advocacy

Legal interpreters are discouraged from performing cultural mediation and absolutely prohibited from performing an advocacy role. This is because of possible legal implications for the interpreter, the attorney, the client and the attorney-client relationship. There is also a potentially disastrous impact on the case and its outcome if the interpreter discusses cultural issues freely or engages in advocacy.

The term "cultural mediation" (also known as culture brokering, intercultural mediation or cultural interpreting) has nothing to do with the legal term "mediation" (as in mediation and arbitration). Around the world, the term mediation refers to the work performed by an interpreter to overcome barriers to communication during or outside an interpreted session. There are many types of mediation, including linguistic mediation (such as clarifying an unfamiliar term), checking for understanding, cultural mediation, client support and advocacy.

During cultural mediation, the interpreter provides general information to the LEP individual or the provider about cultural issues. This activity is permitted in community interpreting, yet many community interpreters have not received in-depth training that would allow them to perform it skillfully and safely. As a result, much confusion has taken place about this practice, and cultural mediation has even been used as a pretext to allow the interpreter to take control of the interpreted encounter in ways that may lead the interpreter to propagate cultural stereotypes, give advice or tell the provider how to handle a situation.

One Cultural Expert's Story

A cultural expert with a PhD in anthropology specialized in the culture of Guatemala. He was asked to serve as an expert witness in an important legal case in the U.S. To the legal team's surprise, he declined the request. When asked about his response, he informed the team that the client came from an indigenous region in Guatemala and he was not competent to discuss the culture of that region. However, he referred the legal team to a colleague who did specialize in that particular region.

In short, cultural mediation and advocacy are among the riskiest activities in any area of interpreting. Interpreters who perform it often do not restrict their comments to objective, commonly accepted cultural information. Certain cultural comments made by interpreters are inappropriate, inaccurate and in some cases even dangerous.

Finally, cultural mediation and advocacy are not universally accepted even for community interpreters. For example, the Healthcare Interpreters Network in Canada issued national standards of practice in 2007 prohibiting community interpreters from engaging in cultural mediation or advocacy. Some hospitals also prohibit healthcare interpreters from engaging in advocacy, and a number of interpreting experts are uneasy with cultural mediation because community interpreters who lack the necessary knowledge and skills to perform it safely and effectively often perform it. Advocacy is a particularly risky activity that makes no sense in legal interpreting, since the client has a staunch advocate in the lawyer.

Specific concerns with cultural mediation in legal interpreting

Legal

- Providing inappropriate cultural information could be construed as giving advice. Giving advice in legal services may constitute practicing law without a license.

- If the interpreter's cultural information proves to be inaccurate, and this information derailed the case, both attorney and interpreter may be liable for the legal consequences to the client. For example, the client could face losing the case, deportation, denial of asylum, or loss of parental rights, income or safety. The client might then sue the attorney and the interpreter.

- By usurping the voice of the client, the interpreter may rob the attorney of an opportunity to hear the client's story in his or her own voice. The attorney thereby loses the ability to competently assess the client and the strength of his/her legal case as well as the ability of the client to communicate appropriately and clearly in a court setting.

Professional

- Interpreters are not anthropologists or sociologists, and the majority of interpreters do not receive formal, in-depth education in cultural issues.

- Culture is complex, not monolithic. It cannot easily be summarized.

- Interpreters are human. Like everyone else, they typically have cultural biases, blind spots and subjective perspectives that skew the cultural information they may provide. Attorneys, however, may trust the interpreters' comments about culture even if they are inaccurate. The attorneys may not verify the information with an expert who could provide a more accurate and objective analysis.

- Interpreters who speak about cultural issues often tend to over-generalize, personalize the information to the client, stereotype the client's ethnic or national group, and/or give subjective opinions. In these and other ways, they inadvertently provide inaccurate information that could have a negative impact on a case.

- Cultural mediation is such a complex skill that few interpreters master it perfectly, making them prone to offer blanket statements or opinions rather than limiting their statements to objective, general, neutral information that includes specific warnings that the information provided may not apply to the client.

The interpreter's culture

- The interpreter may not be from the same country as the client.

- An interpreter from the same country may still be of a different region, social class, educational background, ethnicity, etc., making suspect any cultural assumptions that the interpreter might express about the client.

- The interpreter may be more (or less) acculturated to the U.S. than the client and have no real idea about the client's degree of acculturation, making cultural assumptions again very problematic.

Client-centered practice

- If the interpreter starts giving cultural information, the attorney may look at the interpreter as a source for expertise, eroding the attorney's focus on the client as the trusted source of information.

- Culture is so personal, idiosyncratic and specific that the client is the only reliable source of information on his or her own cultural beliefs and practices: the interpreter may make cultural assumptions that are completely incorrect.

- Once the interpreter has performed a cultural mediation (or other complex mediation), there will be a greater tendency for the client to become more dependent on the interpreter rather than the attorney, and for the attorney to rely on the interpreter's cultural knowledge, potentially undermining the attorney-client relationship.

■ The attorney's questions should be directed to the client, not to the interpreter. Once the interpreter has performed cultural mediation, however, there may be a greater tendency for the lawyer to ask questions of the interpreter that are beyond the interpreter's expertise.

For these and other reasons, cultural mediation (culture brokering) and advocacy are not permitted in legal interpreting.

Modes of Interpreting:
True or False

Circle T for "True" or F for "False"

1. Simultaneous is the mode most commonly used in legal services. T **(F)**

2. Simultaneous mode is preferable as it is more "professional" than consecutive mode. T **(F)**

3. Consecutive mode allows a little more time to process meaning than simultaneous mode. **(T)** F

4. Sight translation is rarely needed in legal services interpreting. T **(F)**

5. Simultaneous interpreting equipment should not be used in non-courtroom legal interpreting. T **(F)**

6. Summary mode is permitted in certain areas of legal services. T **(F)**

7. To save the lawyer's time, sight translation should be executed at the end of the interview after the lawyer has left. T **(F)**

8. Sight translation is important. The interpreter should always perform sight translation when asked to do so by an attorney. **(T)** F

9. Whisper interpreting is a variation of simultaneous mode. T **(F)**

What is the preferred mode of interpreting in non-courtroom legal interpreting, and why is it preferred?

____

____

____

____

When might simultaneous mode be preferred in non-courtroom legal interpreting?

____

____

____

____

Why do many interpreters fail to interrupt a speaker who goes on too long?

____

____

____

____

Pre-Conference

List some of the most important elements that you would include in a pre-conference.

____

____

____

____

Who decides if a pre-conference should be held?

____

____

____

____

Multiple Choice

Circle the correct answer.

1. Legal interpreters who perform linguistic mediation should:

   a. Offer a detailed reason for interrupting the session.

   b. Address the attorney first.

   c. Summarize whatever the attorney answers for the client, to ensure transparency.

   d. Remain in the center until the confusion is resolved.

   e. All of the above.

2. A common error when performing linguistic mediation is:

   a. Failing to interpret the last thing said.

   b. Not identifying oneself as the interpreter.

   c. Using first person ("I noticed a problem and…") instead of third person ("The interpreter would like to request a clarification of…").

   d. All of the above.

3. Of the examples below, the most dangerous risk of performing linguistic mediation is probably:

   a. The interpreter may engage in direct eye contact after performing the mediation.

   b. The interpreter may get caught up in a side conversation.

   c. The interpreter may offer information that is inaccurate and/or inappropriate.

   d. All of the above.

Linguistic Mediation

What are the steps for performing linguistic mediation?

____

____

____

____

How does linguistic mediation relate to mediation in general within the various fields of interpreting?

____

____

____

____

Why shouldn't legal interpreters perform cultural mediation (culture brokering) or advocacy?

____

____

____

____

Who may perform advocacy in legal interpreting? Why?

____

____

____

____

Whom does the interpreter always address first when initiating linguistic mediation? Why?

____

____

____

____

Unit III

INTERPRETING FOR LEGAL SERVICES

The U.S. Legal System

UNIT III, OBJECTIVE 1
Demonstrate knowledge of the U.S. legal system

Understanding the U.S. Legal System

In order to provide effective legal interpreting, the interpreter must understand the nature of the U.S. legal system, the needs of legal services providers and the specific challenges faced by legal interpreters, including terminology.

This unit includes an overview of the U.S. legal system. It also addresses common issues that the interpreter may face in specific areas of law, such as family law or immigration services. In particular, this unit addresses an important challenge that faces interpreters in all areas of law: how to develop and work effectively with legal terminology. An English legal glossary at the end of the manual includes common legal terms with which all legal interpreters should be familiar.

Even when interpreting skills are mastered, legal interpreting remains a fascinating profession in part due to the dramatic and complex nature of law and legal representation. While many lawyers try to speak clearly to their clients, the language of the law can sometimes be technical and daunting. This unit provides practical guidance on how to interpret effectively in legal services.

Definitions

Before entering into a discussion of the U.S. legal system, it will be helpful to preface the discussion with a few important definitions.

American Bar Association (ABA)

The American Bar Association is the largest voluntary professional association in the world. With more than 400,000 members, the ABA provides law school accreditation, continuing legal education, information about the law, programs to assist lawyers and judges in their work, and initiatives to improve the legal system for the public. The ABA has also developed Model Rules of Professional Responsibility (Ethics). With some minor changes, the Rules have been adopted by all states except California, Maine, and New York, which have developed their own rules.

Legal services

Assistance with a legal matter, including giving advice, filing documents, sending letters, and representation in official hearings and other legal proceedings.

Legal services providers

Individuals and organizations that provide legal services. The term is generally used to refer to a non-profit organization, but the term is not exclusive. For-profit providers are generally referred to as law firms.

Unauthorized Practice of Law

Legal services that are not provided in accordance with the relevant Code of Professional Responsibility, or are provided by anyone who is not licensed to practice in that jurisdiction, whether or not they have attended law school or are authorized to practice law elsewhere.

Confidentiality

Practice of treating information as private. Confidentiality is one of the key elements of the attorney-client relationship.

Attorney-client privilege

Protection of confidential communications between a client and her attorney, invoked according to rules of evidence in response to a request, during a court case, for the disclosure of confidential information.

The U.S. Legal System: An Overview

Introduction

An interpreter will not be able to interpret accurately information that she does not understand. It is therefore critical that legal interpreters not only study terminology but also have a good understanding of the context in which the terminology is used. This manual does not attempt to give a comprehensive description of the U.S. legal system, as there are many resources available for that purpose. Interpreters who have not received any formal education on the U.S. government and legal system should seek out such materials before taking any legal interpreting assignments.

This section is intended as a review of some of the peculiarities of the U.S. legal system that may be different from the legal systems of other countries. These differences can greatly confuse many foreign-born participants in the legal system and can also confuse interpreters. Interpreters should be aware of these distinctions to ensure that their interpretations are correct. Word-for-word, or literal, translations of terms from the U.S. legal system into terms in the target language may be inaccurate or misleading if the systems are different.

State vs. Federal – explanation

The United States has adopted a system known as federalism, a balance of power between the federal government and the states. This system is embedded in the U.S. Constitution, which specifies that the federal government reserves certain powers and that any other powers are in the control of the states. Thus, there are Federal and State laws, Federal and State courts, and Federal and State legislatures.

Federal laws generally relate to matters that affect the entire nation and that need to be consistent in all parts of the country to avoid confusion. They may also relate to actions that occur across state lines. Federal issues include immigration, national minimum wage and benefits, and crimes that cross state lines.

States can make their own laws about anything that the Federal government does not control (for example family law) and can also add to Federal laws in a way that is more beneficial to the people residing in that state (for example, creating a local minimum wage that is higher than the Federal minimum wage). This distinction between Federal and State laws can often cause confusion because while some laws (like immigration) are the same in all states, others (like divorce law) are different in each state. Clients who move between states are often confused when they receive different information from different lawyers, or if they are told that a lawyer cannot help the client with a problem that happened in another state.

Civil vs. Criminal Legal Systems

The U.S. divides the legal system into two sections: civil and criminal. There are often separate courts, laws, and rules for each system. A basic comparison of the elements of each system is shown in Table 2.

TABLE 2:
Comparison of Elements in Civil vs. Criminal Legal Systems

Civil System	Criminal System
Cases are filed by an Individual (Plaintiff) against an Individual or Government (Respondent).	Charges are filed by the Government (State or Federal) against an Individual (Defendant).
Either party is allowed to have an attorney, but they must find and pay for their own attorney.	Defendants are provided with a free attorney if they cannot afford to pay for one.
Respondents can be ordered to pay money or take certain actions (e.g., attend counseling, undergo drug testing, rehire an employee who was wrongfully terminated).	Defendants can be sentenced to jail and/or be ordered to pay money or take certain actions; parole and probation may also be ordered.
Generally, there are no immigration consequences to a civil case.	Criminal charges can have immigration consequences, including deportation.

The Civil system governs the interactions between individuals. Common examples of the Civil legal system are employment laws (including laws about minimum wage, discrimination or over-time pay), consumer laws (for example, truth in advertising, bankruptcy and fair lending laws), immigration law and family law (*e.g.*, marriage, child custody or divorce). Civil cases are controlled by the person or government entity that files the case with the court, called the Plaintiff. The Plaintiff will decide what outcome to ask for and can choose to drop the case at any time. A Civil Court generally does not have the power to send anyone to jail.

The Criminal system protects the People (as represented by the Government). Common examples of charges brought in the Criminal legal system are murder, assault, tax evasion, and robbery. The police usually investigate violations of Criminal law, and the case is controlled by the Government (represented by the Prosecutor). The Prosecutor will decide what outcome to ask for, though a judge may impose a more or less harsh punishment. The Prosecutor can choose to drop the case at any time. The victim of the crime is generally asked to serve as a witness for the Prosecutor, but does not actually control the case. A Criminal Court does have the power to send someone to jail, and in some cases can order that a person found guilty be put to death.

Clients are often confused by this system when there are cases pending in both the Civil and Criminal systems related to the same event. For example a victim of domestic violence may be seeking a Protective Order and Child Custody from the Civil Court, while the State's Attorney is pressing charges against the batterer in the Criminal Court (and the victim is asked to testify). Immigrant clients often fear that any interaction with any courts could cause problems with their immigration status, although civil matters generally have no effect on immigration status.

However, it is possible that the Respondent would raise an immigrant's legal status in an attempt at a defense. For example, if the Respondent does not want to pay wages to an employee, the Respondent may point out the fact that the employee is not authorized for employment. In most cases, this is irrelevant, and may cause immigration-related problems for the employer as well – but it is impor-tant to know, as some undocumented individuals may choose not to pursue legal rights out of fear of immigration-related repercussions.

This example illustrates some of the complexity of the U.S. legal system.

The U.S. Congress writes and passes all Immigration laws. These are Federal laws that apply in all states and territories of the U.S. The Department of Homeland Security (DHS), an Administrative Agency, writes the regulations, develops the forms, and grants or denies applications for Immigration relief. Some cases are decided by DHS employees who simply read over the application. Other cases require the immigrant to attend an interview with a DHS employee. If an immigrant is denied relief by the Immigration Courts, she can appeal to the Federal Courts. If she loses her case in the Federal Courts, she has no other options.

Administrative vs. Court

The U.S. government has three branches: Legislative, Executive, and Judicial. Each Branch has an impor-tant role in the legal system. The roles are divided among the three branches in order to balance out the influence of any individual, political party, or branch of the system. The Legislative Branch, which includes the Congress, writes and passes the laws. Once the Legislative Branch has passed laws, they are often sent to the Executive Branch for implementation. The Judicial Branch includes the courts, from the U.S. Supreme Court down to the local county court. The Judicial Branch is in charge of interpretation of the laws and has the final say in any case.

Many laws require implementing regulations that are written by the Executive Branch. These regulations provide the details of how the laws will be enforced (for example, specifying which agency will be responsible for investigating violations or how much the fines will be) or how people can comply with the laws (for example, what forms they will have to submit). The Executive Branch may also establish an administrative court or government agency to oversee the process for compliance with the law. Administrative decisions can generally be appealed to the Judicial Branch. Examples of administrative proceedings include the interviews for immigration benefits like green cards or citizenship carried out by the Bureau of Citizenship and Immigration Services, Social Security Administration applications for SSA benefits, and Health and Human Services interviews to determine eligibility for benefits like food stamps and Medicaid. All of these are administrative, rather than judicial, proceedings.

Most people are more comfortable with an Administrative proceeding than a Court proceeding. Courts are generally more formal and intimidating. Understanding that legal relief can be obtained by simply filing forms or talking with someone in an office can dramatically change a client's interest in pursuing legal remedies.

Trial Court vs. Appellate or Appeals Court

The U.S. legal system is designed to allow for corrections, understanding that mistakes can and will be made within the system. Many legal issues can be resolved through negotiations, resulting in what is often referred to as an out of court settlement. These settlements are often kept confidential. However, if the case goes to a court, it will first go to a trial court. It may be a Civil Court or a Criminal Court, depending on the law involved. The Trial Court is responsible for hearing the evidence in the case (for example, the testimony of witnesses, relevant documents, etc.), and for carefully considering all of the issues and arguments made by both sides. The trial court will then make a decision.

If the losing side of the case is not satisfied with the decision, there is generally a process available to appeal the decision. This is a process of proving to the Appellate Court (a court that hears appeals) that the Trial Court made a mistake or did not know all of the facts. The Appellate Court will typically look at the record of what happened in the Trial Court, before listening to the parties. Other cases are addressed by the Appellate Court "de novo" (which means "anew"), that is, as if there had been no Trial Court decision. There may be several levels of appeal available in a case. The highest Appellate Court in the U.S. is the Supreme Court, but it only accepts a limited number of cases addressing specific legal issues.

The status of a case in this many-layered system can seem deeply confusing. Clients need to understand when a decision is final, and how far an attorney is able or willing to go with their case.

Adversarial vs. Non-Adversarial

Much of the U.S. legal system is designed to be adversarial, meaning that two parties are on opposite sides of the case. In both the Civil and Criminal Legal systems, the adversaries can be referred to as the Plaintiff and the Defendant (or sometimes Petitioner and Respondent in the civil setting). The U.S. system relies on this design to increase the fairness of the legal system. The theory is that both sides present their strongest case and the judge is to decide who is right. The adversaries are expected to be effective in finding all of the facts and in helping to make sure that everyone follows the rules.

However, much of the law happens outside of the courtroom through the application and hearing processes of administrative agencies. Most administrative applications (for example, applications for public benefits) and hearings (for example, interviews for immigration benefits) are conducted without the conventions of the adversarial courtroom. In these settings, the applicant provides information to the administrative agency in order to secure benefits or status, or participates with counsel at a hearing if an initial application is denied. Generally, these processes also include an appeal option, including the possibility of bringing a case in court to reverse the decision.

Most people prefer a non-adversarial process. It is generally less intimidating and stressful. Clients should understand what process they are involved in so that they can be properly prepared, emotionally, for the experience.

The U.S. Legal System and the Interpreter

Clarity about the system

In order to interpret competently, the interpreter will need to understand those aspects of the complex U.S. legal system that are implicated in the lawyer-client communications being interpreted. To this end, the interpreter must clarify with the lawyer whether he or she is talking about federal or state court, judicial vs. administrative proceedings, etc. In addition, during a pre-conference the interpreter may wish to mention to the lawyer that these differences are not clear to many LEP clients.

Attorney-client privilege and confidentiality

While confidentiality is considered an ethical requirement in every sector of interpreting in every part of the world, it has particular importance in legal interpreting. Breaking confidentiality can have a dangerous impact on the outcome of a case. Interpreting for legal services providers increases that risk: the attorney's ethical duty to protect client confidentiality is intended in part to protect the client from harm by ensuring that the client will feel free to be open and honest with his or her attorney. Then the attorney can make strategic decisions and build a stronger case.

Attorney-client privilege is a related issue. By law, information shared with an attorney is protected from discovery by the courts in any legal proceeding, but only if the information has not already been shared. Legal interpreters are included under the confidentiality umbrella of the attorney and covered by the attorney-client privilege for information interpreted for the attorney. Interpreters who reveal confidential information outside the attorney's office, however, or who have side conversations or relationships with the client, may not be protected and may be found to have violated confidentiality and/or privilege.

Unauthorized practice of law (UPL)

The U.S. legal system does not permit anyone but an attorney licensed to practice law in a specific jurisdiction to do so. If the interpreter gives advice, opinions or beliefs to the client, that may constitute the unauthorized practice of law (UPL), and the attorney and interpreter may both be liable for the interpreter's statements. UPL is included within the attorney code of ethics, and some states also have civil or criminal laws regarding UPL.

Liability

The attorney is responsible, and also potentially legally liable, for other aspects of the interpreter's conduct. For example, if the interpreter breaks confidentiality, the client could bring an ethics complaint against the attorney, the interpreter and the attorney's organization, regardless of the outcome of the case.

Legal Services Providers

Description

In criminal court, low-income or indigent defendants are assigned a lawyer by either the court or the public defender's office. In civil cases, low-income litigants will not be assigned a free lawyer but may be able to find one from a legal services provider. In general, three types of legal assistance for low-income clients are widely available in the U.S.:

- Legal aid
- Other nonprofit legal services
- Pro bono attorneys

General Practice Legal Aid Offices

Legal Aid organizations have constituted a particular category of legal assistance for low-income residents since the early 1900's. In 1974, Congress enacted the creation of the Legal Services Corporation (LSC) to disburse funds to legal aid organizations.

> **Legal Assistance**
>
> Civil legal assistance in the United States has, over the last four decades, evolved from a relatively insignificant and disorganized program that provided limited services in only a few areas of the country, with little financial support and political recognition, into a system that provides a broad panoply of legal services to the low-income community nationwide. […] The overarching goal for the civil legal assistance program has always been and will continue to be equal justice for all.
>
> —*Houseman & Perle (2007:49)*

Other nonprofit legal services providers

Hundreds of community-based organizations in the U.S. offer legal services. Some agencies are dedicated to providing legal services to underserved residents of a geographic area. Others focus on a particular group (such as Latinos or Asian Americans/Pacific Islanders). Still other agencies offer a particular type of service, *e.g.*, employment law or immigration services. Such organizations may include legal clinics run out of law schools or may offer mobile services. In some cases, nonprofit organizations with a broader mission also offer legal services. Most provide information, advice and legal representation. Agencies may offer services in one or more of areas of law, including: family law, landlord-tenant disputes, immigration, human rights, consumer protection, and employment law, among others.

Pro bono attorneys

Pro bono (free) legal services are offered by many lawyers and legal staff in the private sector through commercial law firms. The lawyers may do so as volunteers or because they wish to perform pro bono services in response to their ethical obligations, or pro bono service may even be required as a prerequisite to maintaining membership in the state bar. Pro bono attorneys offer their services in a variety of ways. For example, they may:

- Waive their fees for an indigent client who arrives on their doorstep seeking assistance.

- Accept for low cost or no cost low-income clients who are referred by other lawyers or by legal service organizations.

- Participate in organizations that provide or promote pro bono services.

A number of states have established organizations that support pro bono attorneys. Many legal service agencies also provide training and mentoring for pro bono attorneys in private practice.

Self-help clinics

These clinics may be sponsored by local and county bar associations or other groups and held in senior centers, immigration service sites and many other settings. Volunteer lawyers help out with legal forms, provide legal advice and answer questions. The clinics may be regular, episodic or annual. Sometimes the meetings with an attorney are one-on-one, but the attorney may also work with a small group.

Courthouse facilitators

A growing number of local courthouses offer facilitators who help individuals without attorneys to process legal claims and file legal paperwork. They may also explain the legal process. (Some may be called court facilitators, family law facilitators, or family court facilitators.) Many of their services are free, but some counties charge for the service. In addition, such programs may sell legal forms and "do-it-yourself" legal kits (*e.g.*, for divorce). Although many offices operate on a walk-in basis, others require appointments. In addition to identifying required forms and reviewing forms, facilitators may make referrals to other agencies or help schedule hearings. In general they are not permitted to provide legal advice or to provide legal representation.

Other legal programs

If a client does not qualify for free legal services yet does not have enough funds to hire an attorney, some legal programs and hotlines offer low-cost or sliding-fee services that charge by the minute. Others may offer a flat fee for the legal service. Such programs may be operated not only by nonprofit agencies but by private law firms.

Areas of Law Covered by Non-Profit Legal Services

Those who interpret for legal services providers will often be asked to interpret in the following areas of law:

- Employment law (*e.g.*, employment discrimination, mandatory overtime with no pay, unpaid wages, worker's compensation)

- Immigration (*e.g.*, applications for permanent residence, naturalization, work permits, asylum, trafficking visas)

- Family law (*e.g.*, divorce, child custody, loss of parental rights, child support)

- Domestic violence (*e.g.*, protective orders, self-petitions to obtain permanent residence, access to housing/benefits)

- Consumer law (*e.g.*, scam victims, reducing major medical bills, predatory lending or fraud)

- Public benefits (*e.g.*, loss or termination of benefits like food stamps, obtaining emergency medical assistance, subsidized housing, eligibility of lawful permanent residents vs. citizens)

- Landlord-tenant disputes (*e.g.*, unlawful evictions, eviction notices, rental discrimination, overcrowding, lease violations)

Legal Concepts

Many LEP clients lack an understanding of basic legal concepts in the U.S. because there may not be an exact conceptual or legal equivalent in the client's language. Examples may include:

- Constitutional rights
- Legal services providers (in particular, the concept of free lawyers)
- Right to counsel
- Jury (and the concept of being tried by a jury of one's peers)
- Presumption of innocence
- Parole
- Probation
- The concept of "confronting one's accusers"
- Protection orders
- Minimum wage
- Adjustable rate mortgage
- Overtime
- Compensatory damages
- Liquidated damages

In situations like this, the interpreter may have to perform linguistic mediation so that the attorney can check for understanding or clarify a concept. *The interpreter should never try to clarify a legal term or concept, even during linguistic mediation.* Instead, the interpreter could say something like the following to the attorney and then the client:

- Excuse me, but the interpreter would like to point out that she is unable to interpret the term "protection order" as it has no exact equivalent in Twi [or the target language].
- The interpreter has interpreted the term "compensatory damages" literally. However, to the interpreter's knowledge, this term does not have a standard meaning in [the target language], so perhaps it will not be clearly understood.

Statements of this kind allow the attorney an opportunity to clarify the legal term or concept for the client. They also alert the attorney to the fact that such issues may also arise in other languages.

Attorney-Client Relationships

Lawyers who choose to work for nonprofit legal services are typically committed to providing exemplary service, even for clients who cannot afford to pay. The conduct of such lawyers is governed by more than ethical considerations: their personal values and social justice mission may also influence their work. Lawyers in legal services may not fully understand the cultural or linguistic complexities of their clients' cases, but they do wish to provide competent legal assistance to all clients.

It is vital that interpreters support the work of the attorneys. One of the best ways that an interpreter can support lawyers serving Deaf or LEP individuals is for the interpreter to become familiar with, understand and respect the attorney-client relationship, including the ethical rules that govern it.

As part of professional respect for legal services providers and the legal profession itself, the interpreter should make an effort to understand the profession of law and lawyers' ethical requirements.

Ethical Obligations for Lawyers

Attorneys take their ethical obligations seriously. It is important for interpreters in legal services to acquire a deep understanding of the attorney-client relationship and the ethical rules that govern it so that the interpreter's conduct does not violate the lawyer's canon of legal ethics or undermine the client's interests.

As a condition of obtaining and maintaining their license to practice law, lawyers are bound by rules of professional conduct promulgated by the highest court of the jurisdictions in which they practice. While important differences exist in the rules of different states, most are patterned on the American Bar Association's (ABA) Model Rules of Professional Conduct, or the predecessor of that document, the ABA Model Code of Professional Responsibility. For example, the Court of Appeals of the District of Columbia has issued the D.C. Rules of Professional Conduct, accessible at **www.dcbar.org**, which are based on the ABA Model Rules. California and Maine are the only states that have developed their own rules, independent of the ABA. In addition, immigration courts (under the Executive Office for Immigration Review) have adopted their own ethical rules. Interpreters may wish to consult the rules of the jurisdiction or area for which they are interpreting.

Consulting the rules of particular jurisdictions may be challenging for interpreters in areas with small states, where the same legal interpreter could easily interpret in several contiguous states, *e.g.*, the District of Columbia, Maryland, Virginia and Delaware or Pennsylvania. (Some interpreters, both for Spanish and for languages of limited diffusion, as well as federally court-certified interpreters, may interpret in quite a number of different states across the U.S.) Attorneys, however, must follow the rules for the court in which a case will be heard. As with the D.C. Rules, the state's rules are often published on the state bar association's website.

To consult the complete ABA Model Rules, including discussion and commentary, see **www. abanet.org/cpr/mrpc/mrpc_toc.html** at the ABA website. The interpreter is encouraged to read this code in its entirety, as it is a vital and illuminating document. The highlights offered here do not render it justice, and the commentary included is intended only to underscore areas of the Model Rules most relevant to the legal interpreter and offer a general sense of the lawyer's ethical obligations.

Interpreters working, for example, in Washington, D.C., should also review the D.C. Rules of Professional Conduct, available at the District of Columbia Bar website, **www.dcbar.org**.

ABA Model Rules of Professional Conduct

Overview of the Rules

The ABA Model Rules, subject to some modification, have become the rules of most licensing jurisdictions. Lawyers are required to adhere to the rules of the jurisdiction where cases will be heard. Violation of these rules can result in discipline, including disbarment.

It is important that the interpreter never act in a way that contradicts the lawyer's rules of conduct because, as has been stated often in this manual, the attorney may be held ethically and legally liable for the interpreter's conduct.

In general, most jurisdictions adhere to the following ABA Model Rules, meaning that Deaf or LEP clients in legal services, like all clients, can and should expect that the attorney (often with the support of an interpreter) will:

- Treat the client with courtesy and respect the client's dignity.

- Endeavor to handle every case competently and diligently.

- Communicate clearly and respond promptly to client requests.

- Charge reasonable fees, if any, and explain clearly, in advance, how they are calculated. (Note that most legal services providers for low-income clients charge low fees or no fees and attempt to have court costs and other fees waived.)

- Keep client information strictly confidential.

- Avoid conflicts of interest.

- Provide a client with an informed understanding of the client's legal rights and obligations.

- Act as a zealous advocate for the client's position and seek a result advantageous to the client.

- Exercise sensitive professional and moral judgment.

- Keep the client informed, including providing copies of important papers.

- Exhibit a high level of ethical conduct.

In addition to the Rules above, the ABA amplifies the discussion in a "preamble and scope" document available at **www.abanet.org**. Note that a lawyer who violates the Rules of Professional Conduct could face a disciplinary process and may be sanctioned for such a violation, up to and including the loss of the attorney's license to practice law.

Summary of the ABA Model Rules

Rule 1.1. Competence

A lawyer shall provide competent representation to a client.

Rule 1.2 Scope of Representation

…A lawyer shall abide by a client's decisions … and … shall consult with the client as to the means by which they are to be pursued.

Rule 1.3 Diligence

A lawyer shall act with reasonable diligence and promptness in representing a client.

Rule 1.4 Communications

… A lawyer shall… keep the client reasonably informed about the status of the matter.

Rule 1.5 Fees

.. A lawyer shall not make an agreement for, charge, or collect an unreasonable fee. … The fee and expenses … shall be communicated to the client, preferably in writing.

Rule 1.6 Confidentiality of Information

…(a) A lawyer shall not reveal information relating to the representation of a client unless the client gives informed consent,… or the disclosure is permitted by paragraph (b)[except] […] (b) A lawyer may reveal information relating to the representation of a client

to the extent the lawyer reasonably believes necessary: (1) to prevent reasonably certain death or substantial bodily harm; (2) to prevent the client from committing a crime or fraud… (3) to prevent, mitigate or rectify substantial injury to the financial interests or property of another…; (4) to secure legal advice about the lawyer's compliance with these Rules; (5) to establish a claim or defense on behalf of the lawyer in a controversy between the lawyer and the client …; or (6) to comply with other law or a court order.

Rule 1.7 Conflict of Interest: Current Clients

…A lawyer shall not represent a client if the representation involves a concurrent conflict of interest.

(Rules 1.8 through 1.18 are not quoted here, as they may be of less relevance to the interpreter.)

Confidentiality

One of the ABA Model Rules is particularly important and relevant for legal interpreters. It should be carefully noted.

Rule 1.6 Confidentiality

a. A lawyer shall not reveal information relating to the representation of a client unless the client gives informed consent, the disclosure is impliedly authorized in order to carry out the representation or the disclosure is permitted by paragraph (b).

b. A lawyer may reveal information relating to the representation of a client to the extent the lawyer reasonably believes necessary:

1. to prevent reasonably certain death or substantial bodily harm;

2. to prevent the client from committing a crime or fraud that is reasonably certain to result in substantial injury to the financial interests or property of another and in furtherance of which the client has used or is using the lawyer's services;

3. to prevent, mitigate or rectify substantial injury to the financial interests or property of another that is reasonably certain to result or has resulted from the client's c ommission of a crime or fraud in further- ance of which the client has used the lawyer's services;

4. to secure legal advice about the lawyer's compliance with these Rules;

5. to establish a claim or defense on behalf of the lawyer in a controversy between the lawyer and the client, to establish a defense to a criminal charge or civil claim against the lawyer based upon conduct in which the client was involved, or to respond to allegations in any proceeding concerning the lawyer's representation of the client; or

6. to comply with other law or a court order.

Challenges in Legal Interpreting

Broadly speaking, there are at least three main types of challenges that face legal interpreters:

- Physical and other conditions
- Attorney and client expectations
- Individual/personal and organizational culture (including the professional culture of the legal services provider)

Individual conditions can be variable. Perhaps a nonprofit legal services agency is located in an old building whose air conditioning is so loud that it interferes with the interpreter's ability to hear and concentrate. Or perhaps the interpreter arrives and finds that she and the client do not really speak the same language or dialect.

Certain lawyer or client expectations may be more predictable. It is common, for example, that some attorneys who are not accustomed to working with professional interpreters may unintentionally expect interpreters to violate their ethical canons (*e.g.*, by allowing the interpreter to give advice or to perform sight translation without a lawyer present). Clients, too, may have unreasonable expectations: they often want to ask the interpreter questions about their case in private because they trust the interpreter's opinion.

Individual culture, whether the client's or the lawyer's, is another frequent challenge that was discussed in Unit II. But organizational culture, like personal culture, can be a challenge, too. In general, there will be a common expectation by many in the nonprofit legal culture that the interpreter's job is to "help out," or be "a part of the team," with the idea in mind that the interpreter can and should provide services beyond interpreting. Consequently, it may be necessary for the interpreter to clarify the interpreter's exact role.

Similarly, some lawyers may expect the interpreter to perform inappropriate or risky tasks, such as helping the client fill out forms while the interpreter is alone with the client. They may ask the interpreter to call clients to relay information about the case. Some attorneys have asked interpreters to drive to the client's house to drop off information. It is the interpreter's responsibility to meet such challenges while adhering to interpreter ethics. At the same time, the interpreter can work with legal service providers to assure that the provider and client communicate effectively.

Legal Services Interpreting

The following examples include general concerns for interpreters in legal services followed by challenges specific to certain types of services.

Conditions

- Terminology. The challenge of learning basic legal terminology exists in virtually every sector of legal interpreting (and, for that matter, every other sector of interpreting). Each type of service has its own terms, jargon, acronyms and abbreviations.

- Formality. Interpreting in any legal setting is formal. The interpreter's role in this regard is to discourage personal or casual relationships or discussions with clients or legal services staff.

- Physical working conditions. Some legal services nonprofits operate in physical conditions that might include possible challenges like cramped offices, crying babies or background interference.

- Language/dialect/regional variations. The interpreter may arrive and find that he or she cannot communicate with the client effectively because the interpreter and client do not share a common language.

Expectations

- Lawyers and clients often expect the interpreter should do more than simply interpret, *e.g.*, give advice, make phone calls, drop off paperwork, drive the client to a next appointment, etc.

- Legal staff members often expect interpreters to translate documents.

- Clients may appeal to interpreters' heartstrings and ask them to sight translate bills or correspondence, make phone calls, fix problems, give referrals to other services, etc. They may expect the interpreter to become a friend and confidante, give advice about the quality of the legal services, or assist the client in making a decision about legal options.

- Some lawyers may expect interpreters to have social services expertise and function as de facto case managers for their clients.

- Lawyers who have worked with untrained interpreters may expect the legal interpreter to behave in many of the same ways that an untrained interpreter might do: "Well, So-and-so does what I ask. Why don't you?"

- No-shows/late-shows. Some clients may believe it is all right to come two hours late or not at all. This problem affects the interpreter, who arrives punctually and may not be able to stay late due to scheduled assignments.

Systemic Culture

- Few legal services providers encountered by the interpreter have been trained to work with interpreters.

- Many legal services agencies are not aware of appropriate interpreting ethics, protocols and procedures.

- Some clients may have low levels of education and various degrees of acculturation to the U.S., making it difficult for them to understand the legal system and its culture.

- Lawyers assume that clients must understand what they are being told, thinking that otherwise the clients would ask questions. The interpreter, on the other hand, might suspect that the client's cultural background may impede them from asking questions, for example, due to respect for authority figures.

- The law is intimidating. The law is also culturally different from country to country (and often operates differently for different segments of society within the same country). This complexity combined with fear may render some clients silent and uncommunicative with their legal services provider, who may not understand the cause of their lack of communication, leading to frustration with the client.

Special note: *Challenges related to individual/ personal culture were addressed in Unit II.*

Specific Areas of Law

The following examples are given only as illustrations of common concerns in particular areas of law.

Immigration

- Asylum cases. Many asylum cases include stories of torture, abuse, rape, war trauma and other violent and extreme stories.

- Deportation. The interpreter may see whole families about to be deported, or families broken up by deportation, which can be deeply disturbing.

- Acronyms. While all areas of legal interpreting involve acronyms, the immigration field seems particularly rich in them. Legal forms are often referred to by their numbers, *e.g.*, the N-400 (application for naturalization).

- Clients frequently ask interpreters for immigration advice. *Never answer a question about immigration matters.* Immigration is a specialized area of law.

Family Law

- Impartiality. In common matters like divorce and child custody, if the interpreter has had a similar experience it may have an impact on impartiality.

- Fear. Many parents are terrified of losing their children or being deported in cases of divorce.

Domestic Violence/Sexual Assault

- Safety. Interpreters should engage in safety planning if necessary and speak to the attorney about personal safety. The attorney will typically be aware if there is a risk that the abuser may know the interpreter.

- Stress. The interpreter will hear difficult stories that may cause secondary trauma that can result in interpreter burnout.

- Home numbers. Interpreters have been tempted to give personal numbers in cases of domestic violence.

- Frustration. If a client ends up going back to the abuser (as often happens), the interpreter who has become emotionally involved may feel angry, frustrated or worried.

- Boundary issues. If the client is weeping, reaching out to hold the client's hand, and providing comfort can make it difficult to maintain boundaries.

- Hours. For example, a lawyer might request that an interpreter help a client obtain an Emergency Protective Order after work hours.

- Personal experience. Some studies estimate that 1 in 3 or 4 women in America has been sexually assaulted, and one in 10 has been abused, so it is likely that some interpreters may have personal experiences or memories that might be triggered by interpreting in a domestic violence or sexual assault case.

Landlord-Tenant

- Clients who face eviction for nonpayment of rent are summoned to court on short notice. The fear of the court proceeding and the potential loss of scarce shelter contribute to a stressful situation.

- Clients may be frustrated by their landlords' failure to correct hazardous conditions. They may not understand that the law allows landlords to take them to court for nonpayment of rent, even if they are withholding rent to force landlords to honor their obligation to make repairs.

- Clients may be afraid to allow housing inspectors into their apartments to report housing code violations, even though the inspectors' reports document those violations.

Employment Law

- Numbers. In some cases, a large group of employees (50 or more) may be involved.

Challenges Common to Several Areas of Law

- Complexity of terminology.

- Emotional intensity.

- Possibility of anger, coarse language and high-running emotions.

- Feelings of personal involvement/empathy/ sympathy on the interpreter's part.

- Frustration for the interpreter if things go badly.

- Vicarious trauma.

- Personal biases of the interpreter (*e.g.*, toward clients' odors/hygiene, toward the discriminatory attitudes against LEP individuals of some public benefits providers or regarding persons with less education than the interpreter).

In some cases, the interpreter may need to withdraw from a case if s/he becomes emotionally involved. If the interpreter feels vicarious or secondary trauma and starts to experience stress, nightmares or burnout, it may be necessary to decline assignments or take special measures for self care, including counseling. In addition, because interpreters, like all human beings, have personal biases, they should attend training in cultural competence or cultural diversity to help them identify their biases and minimize the impact on interpreted sessions. This will help prevent unconscious biases from having an inadvertent negative affect on the accuracy or quality of interpreting.

Attorneys *and* Clients

As almost any interpreter can attest, requests for an interpreter to do something other than interpret are common, whether they come from clients or service providers.

Sometimes the requests are appropriate (*e.g.*, an attorney's request for the interpreter to listen to a client's speech to make sure that the dialect/regional variation is a good match for the interpreter's language skills). Sometimes the requests are inappropriate (for example, a request from a client to have the interpreter assist the client with a private matter).

Inappropriate requests place a burden on the interpreter. They can create an uncomfortable situation, whether they come from the lawyer or the client. For example, interpreters who come from less assertive cultures may find it difficult to say no to figures of authority, including attorneys. Saying "no" can feel particularly difficult if the attorney or client exerts pressure on the interpreter or becomes aggressive about the request.

Turning down a client request can also be difficult for an interpreter if the interpreter is from the same culture, because there may be a cultural expectation that the interpreter should "help" the client. Some common situations created by inappropriate requests are illustrated in the following examples.

Requests from the Client

Note that the solutions below are merely lists of suggestions. The interpreter is not expected to engage in all the recommended solutions, but rather use those that make sense in a particular situation.

1. *Role boundary violations:* Requests to perform personal services (*e.g.*, sight translating correspondence, driving the client somewhere, making phone calls) can erode boundaries and blur the interpreter's role. This is particular true for bilingual employees who interpret.

Consequences: Agreeing to perform personal services for clients increases the risk that the interpreter will be alone with the client, engage in personal communications, influence a client's decision-making about his or her case and inadvertently offer opinions or advice to the client that may constitute the unauthorized practice of law. Performing personal services for a client often promotes client dependency. The interpreter may learn too much about the client and feel compromised, for example, if the client later lies to the lawyer (and the interpreter knows it). The client may disclose critical information during one of these side activities. Since the disclosure was not within the attorney-client relationship, it may not be covered by attorney-client privilege. If knowledge about the interpreter's inappropriate activities with the clients becomes known, the interpreter could be forced to testify against the client and undermine the case and/or lose her certification and credibility. Attorney-client privilege may potentially be compromised any time that the interpreter becomes an active participant and/or the attorney is not present when his or her client has communication with the interpreter.

Solutions: Clarify the interpreter's role (respecting transparency if the client's request or question occurs during the session). Cite the interpreter's code of ethics. Conduct oneself with professionalism: dress, behave and speak in a somewhat formal way. Use the formal mode of address in languages that have one. Use titles such as Mr. and Mrs. and offer only your last name. Seek support from legal services staff to assert boundaries. Explain potential legal consequences to the client of any personal involvement with the client by the interpreter. Mention the need for the interpreter to withdraw from the case if the interpreter is no longer impartial. Explain the dangers for the interpreter of knowing too much. Refer the client to the attorney or the front desk of the legal services agency to request additional assistance.

2. *Requests for advice:* The client often asks the interpreter, "What do you think I should do?" "What do you think about this?" "Where is my case going?" The answers to these questions may constitute legal advice. Responding to such requests violates the interpreter's ethical canons on impartiality, conflicts of interest and scope of practice. The interpreter is prohibited from answering such questions.

Consequences: If the interpreter gives advice, she may violate the interpreter's code of ethics and engage in illegal behavior (unauthorized practice of law). The interpreter is also no longer impartial and will invite more and more dependent behavior from this and other clients. The interpreter could be prosecuted. The attorney could be disbarred (lose his or her license to practice law). The client may follow the interpreter's advice and suffer great harm (such as loss of money, deportation or physical injury).

Solutions: Always refer requests from a client for advice back to the attorney. Be clear about limitations on the interpreter's role. Explain that interpreters are not licensed to practice law. Cite the interpreter's code of ethics. Remain firm that giving advice is forbidden to interpreters. Explain the serious consequences for both the client and the interpreter for soliciting or receiving legal advice from the interpreter. Point out that the interpreter could lose her certification and her work as an interpreter as a result of giving advice. Mention the cultural importance in the U.S. of client autonomy and self-determination. Emphasize the dangers of meddling, since the client will bear the legal consequences of his or her decisions. Make it clear that educating the client about the legal system (or whatever the client is asking about) is the attorney's job, not the interpreter's. Reconnect the client either to the attorney or to other legal services staff for additional guidance. Cite the interpreter's legal liability if she gives advice.

Requests from the Attorney

1. *Requests to perform duties in the absence of the attorney.* The lawyer requests that the interpreter perform a sight translation, help fill out forms, explain a document and so forth while the lawyer leaves to do something else. When the attorney leaves the client and interpreter alone, the interpreter is exposed to the client, who often asks questions of the interpreter although the interpreter is not permitted to answer those questions.

Consequences: The interpreter may be tempted to violate the code of ethics if left alone with the client. The client who cannot ask her attorney questions (and has forgotten them when the attorney returns) may be misinformed, make poor decisions or misunderstand the case. The case may then move off track and result in an unjust outcome. The attorney and interpreter may be legally liable for errors resulting from such a situation. Also, if left alone with the client, the interpreter may be pressured to respond to inappropriate requests or questions from the client.

Solutions: Be polite but firm that the attorney must be present for all tasks performed by the interpreter. Clarify the role and limitations of the legal interpreter. Cite the interpreter code of ethics. Leave the room when the attorney leaves. Calmly and professionally provide reasons for the dangerous consequences and legal liability arising from an interpreter being left alone with the client. Cite examples of possible problems that may arise. Explain that clients who know they will be alone with the interpreter often save their questions for the interpreter rather than asking their attorneys. Emphasize that the relationship of trust must be built between the attorney and client, yet leaving the client alone with the interpreter tends to undermine that relationship in favor of the client-interpreter relationship. This problem occurs because clients tend to trust interpreters, in part because the two speak the same language and often come from similar cultures. Suggest alternatives, *e.g.*, having the interpreter perform the sight translation at the next appointment, or waiting until the attorney is free to return to perform it.

2. *Requests for translation of documents.* The lawyer asks the interpreter to translate a document. The interpreter is not qualified to do so; however, perhaps this is a first assignment at that agency and the interpreter does not want to say no or give a negative impression. Accepting the request, however, would violate the ethical canon on Scope of Practice (if the interpreter is not a trained, qualified legal translator).

Consequences: By translating the document, the interpreter may violate the code of ethics and also produce an unprofessional and dangerously inaccurate document. Such errors often offend literate native speakers who read the poor translations. The agency's reputation among speakers of the language could be lowered. The interpreter's professionalism and reputation could be undermined if word gets out regarding an inaccurate translation. The lawyer, not realizing the problem, may expect all interpreters to perform legal translations. The interpreter may not be appropriately compensated, since few people outside the field of translation understand how long it takes to perform a professional translation. The interpreter may feel pressured or harassed into agreeing. Agreeing to translate makes it harder for other interpreters to decline such requests. The translation will not be adequate or accurate, and so a case may be lost due to a lack of evidence, or false or conflicting evidence (if the inaccurate translation submitted for the case conflicts with other evidence submitted).

Solutions: Cite the interpreter code of ethics. State the interpreter's exact credentials. Explain which credentials and practices attest to a translator's qualifications and experience: *e.g.*, training or education in translation; experience working as part of a professional team that includes two translators (one to translate, one to review) and a proofreader; a high level of language proficiency as assessed by a validated test; and certification by NAJIT or by the American Translators Association (ATA) into the translator's native language or "language of habitual use."* Emphasize that the repercussions of inaccurate translations can be legal and dangerous, and also that poor translations reflect poorly on the credibility of the legal services organization. Recommend that the organization use a professional language services agency and check the qualifications of its translators or look for local certified translators using the database accessible on the website of NAJIT (**www.najit. org**) or ATA (**www.atanet.org**).

---

* For translation, it is unusual to be equally competent at translating in both directions. The ATA certification program reflects this reality. Certification is awarded separately, for example, for German-to-English and for English-to-German, following two different certification tests, because typically there is a significant difference between how well one can translate into and out of a language. It is not permissible under ATA rules to state that one is a "certified translator of German." Instead, one must state the direction as well as the language pair, *e.g.*, "ATA-certified German>English."

Legal Terminology

Many interpreters come to legal interpreter training hoping that attending the training program will provide them with an in-depth knowledge of legal terminology.

Unfortunately, acquiring proficiency in terminology can take years, and interpreters must continuously strive to enhance their vocabulary. This effort requires steady work and practice. It cannot be accomplished during a single training. The legal interpreter will have to prepare carefully for each assignment.

That said, the more terminology that the interpreter acquires, the more confidence he or she develops. Acquiring strong skills in terminology also increases the interpreter's sense of professionalism and self-respect. It is usually easy to tell which interpreters have studied their terminology: they tend to carry and present themselves more professionally. They also appear more secure in their role.

The interpreter reaps many rewards for studying terminology, but perhaps the most important is the degree to which this type of study helps the interpreter to perform the job accurately and, in doing so, support equal access to justice.

Strategies for Developing Legal Terminology

Effective strategies used by many legal interpreters to develop, maintain and expand their legal terminology include the following:

General Strategies

- Obtain the following dictionaries, if possible:
  - A *comprehensive* monolingual dictionary for each working language. It should be more extensive than a "collegiate" dictionary.
  - A monolingual legal dictionary, preferably in each of the interpreter's working languages (see Appendix 2 for sample listings).
  - A bilingual legal dictionary.
- Consider purchasing legal terminology software or subscribe to an online terminology service.
- Purchase a multilingual hand-held electronic dictionary.
- Collect appropriate glossaries for specific sectors of legal terminology that you interpret for or are likely to interpret for.
- Memorize 5 (or any number of) new terms per day from these glossaries.
- Carry a small notebook to note down new legal terms that arise.
- Use self-study resources (see Appendix 2 for examples).
- Watch TV court, legal shows, news and general talk shows in all your working languages: write down new terms as you listen and look them up later.
- Practice simultaneous interpreting while listening to such shows to become comfortable interpreting legal situations.
- Ask other interpreters what general strategies work for them.
- Use websites such as **www.wordreference.com** to find words that are not available in your dictionary (see Appendix 2 for glossary/online dictionary sites).
- Join a translators forum such as **www.proz.com** or a language forum such as **http://forum.wordreference.com**. Post questions.
- Attend public court proceedings in the areas of law you are likely to interpret for and see how difficult it would be to interpret; practice silent simultaneous interpreting while there.

Preparing for Assignments

Before proceeding to an interpreted assignment, the interpreter should obtain as much information as possible about the encounter, including the client's name if possible, the client's country of origin and preferred language/dialect/regional variation, the type of legal service involved, the nature of the session, any relevant documents and any specific terminology that might be required.

In addition the interpreter may:

- Obtain brochures from the relevant legal service provider and note any new terminology.

- Ask the attorney to provide ahead of time the relevant documents (especially those that you will be asked to sight translate or will be directly referenced during the assignment).

- Check for online glossaries specific to the relevant sector of terminology.

- Study the particular area of legal service in articles in Wikipedia, now available in over 200 languages.

- Read articles online relevant to a particular area of law and note any new terms.

- Build a bilingual glossary for a particular area of law by adding from various sources, then creating a Word document (or other format) to save it and use it/add to it for the future.

- Call another interpreter who has interpreted for that agency and ask for advice/guidance about terminology issues.

- Ask the assigning interpreter service for suggestions; they may have in-house terminology resources.

- SELF-TEST: before the assignment, take your mini-glossary for that legal service, cover up the column with the terms in the weaker language and check what you know. Cross out the terms you did knew well and try again with those you did not, until you know all the terms for that glossary.

- Have a friend test you by asking you legal terms at random from a list for you to interpret into the target language.

Nowadays, many legal interpreters will text-message each other with questions, check online glossaries using their laptops or PDAs (with translation software installed), or use electronic hand-held dictionaries during a session. In these and other ways, interpreters are bringing the technology of interpreting into the 21st century.

Professional Development

Almost any training in legal terminology will help to enhance terminology skills. But there are other ways to pursue general professional development, which will, by extension, increase the interpreter's knowledge, and appropriate usage, of legal terminology. For example, the interpreter could:

- Become a member of NAJIT (**www.najit.org**), the professional association for legal interpreters and translators. Join the NAJIT listserv, which often discusses terminology and related issues. You may also pose queries to the listserv if a particular term is not found in your dictionary. In addition, NAJIT offers workshops around the country as well as language-specific skills building in languages other than Spanish.

- Join the American Translators Association (**www. atanet.org**), which offers seminars and conferences all across the country, including many workshops on court and legal interpreting, as well as language-specific peer groups for interpreters and translators, listservs and newsletters

- Spanish interpreters could attend a three-week summer training at the University of Arizona Agnes Haury Institute for Court Interpretation (**http://nci.arizona.edu/ahi.html**), the longest running intensive Spanish/English interpreter training program in the United States. It is currently in its 24th year.

- The Monterey Institute of International Studies, which offers perhaps the most prestigious graduate programs for interpreters in the U.S., now offers shorter programs on interpreting, particularly for Spanish, as well as a train-the-trainer program for interpreter trainers in all areas of interpreting. See **http://translate.miis.edu/ndp/ programs.html** for details and programs.

- Join an online translators' forum. A growing number of them exist. For example, a legal translators' forum that covers many languages is run through Yahoo groups at **http://finance.groups. yahoo.com/group/legaltranslators/**.

Resources for Terminology

For a detailed list of terminology resources for
legal interpreters, see Appendix 2 of this manual.
The list includes:

- Resources for self-study
- Dictionaries and legal glossaries
- Dictionary software
- Online legal dictionaries and glossaries (English and multilingual)
- Online general dictionaries (English and multilingual)
- International book distributors
- Resources for legal translators

In Conclusion

This manual represents a new approach to training
legal interpreters who work primarily outside the
courtroom in nonprofit legal services. While the
focus of this program is attorney-client interviews,
the information presented here is largely applicable
to nearly any area of non-courtroom legal interpreting. However, the information will be most helpful
for legal interpreters who perform interview interpreting in collaborative settings.

The field of legal interpreting has evolved rapidly
and will continue to do so. This manual is intended
to support legal interpreters and guide them to
perform their vital work safely, professionally and
appropriately. By supporting legal interpreters, the
program may help them to enhance their work and
thereby promote equal access to justice for all.

Unit III Review

The U.S. Legal System

Give three examples of what might make the U.S. legal system appear daunting or confusing to many Deaf or LEP clients of legal services.

____

____

____

____

What are three important points that any legal interpreter should know about the U.S. legal system?

____

____

____

____

Standards of Practice

Review the information on standards in this unit and answer the following questions:

Circle the correct answer.

1. Legal interpreters must:

   a. Interpret words like "yeah" and "um" exactly as they are said.

   b. Avoid using first person wherever possible.

   c. Give cultural information.

   d. None of the above.

   e. All of the above.

2. No matter how it may upset the interpreter, the interpreter must always interpret:

   a. Sexual terms.

   b. Racial or ethnic insults.

   c. Coarse language and obscenities.

   d. Some of the above.

   e. All of the above.

3. Notes containing sensitive or confidential information taken by the interpreter in legal services should be:

   a. Destroyed before leaving the agency.

   b. Destroyed after leaving the agency.

   c. Left with the attorney.

   d. Locked up by the interpreter in a secure location.

Requests

Give three examples of *appropriate* requests (from either a client or an attorney) that an interpreter may reasonably assist with (such as sight translation of a consent form), and three examples of *inappropriate* requests (such as the request for the interpreter to tell an attorney whether a client is mentally competent) that the interpreter should respectfully decline. Do not use the two examples above.

____

____

____

____

____

____

____

____

Write down strong arguments for the following:

1. Why should the interpreter not translate a legal document?

____

____

____

____

____

____

2. In such a case, what could the interpreter suggest instead?

____

____

____

____

____

____

3. Why should the interpreter who performs sight translation for a client never be left alone by the lawyer or legal services provider?

____

____

____

____

____

____

4. Think of alternatives to suggest for that request (*e.g.,* "I would be happy to come back early for the next appointment if you would like me to sight translate this document then.").

____

____

____

____

____

5. When might it be acceptable for an interpreter to translate a legal document? (Focus on the interpreter's qualifications.)

____

____

____

____

____

____

Terminology

How would you prepare for an upcoming session in an area of law for which you have never interpreted before?

____

____

____

____

____

What do you plan to do to enhance your legal terminology after this program?

____

____

____

____

____

____

____

Appendices

Appendix 1

NCSC Model Code of Professional Responsibility for Interpreters in the Judiciary

Only the 10 canons are included below. For the complete code and commentary, please go to **http://www.ncsconline.org/wc/publications/Res_CtInte_ModelGuideChapter9Pub.pdf.**

Canon 1: Accuracy and Completeness

Interpreters shall render a complete and accurate interpretation or sight translation, without altering, omitting, or adding anything to what is stated or written, and without explanation.

Canon 2: Representation of Qualifications

Interpreters shall accurately and completely represent their certifications, training, and pertinent experience.

Canon 3: Impartiality and Avoidance of Conflict of Interest

Interpreters shall be impartial and unbiased and shall refrain from conduct that may give an appearance of bias. Interpreters shall disclose any real or perceived conflict of interest.

Canon 4: Professional Demeanor

Interpreters shall conduct themselves in a manner consistent with the dignity of the court and shall be as unobtrusive as possible.

Canon 5: Confidentiality

Interpreters shall protect the confidentiality of all privileged and other confidential information.

Canon 6: Restriction of Public Comment

Interpreters shall not publicly discuss, report, or offer an opinion concerning a matter in which they are or have been engaged, even when that information is not privileged or required by law to be confidential.

Canon 7: Scope of Practice

Interpreters shall limit themselves to interpreting or translating, and shall not give legal advice, express personal opinions to individuals for whom they are interpreting, or engage in any other activities which may be construed to constitute a service other than interpreting or translating while serving as an interpreter.

Canon 8: Assessing and Reporting Impediments to Performance

Interpreters shall assess at all times their ability to deliver their services. When interpreters have any reservation about their ability to satisfy an assignment competently, they shall immediately convey that reservation to the appropriate judicial authority.

Canon 9: Duty to Report Ethical Violations

Interpreters shall report to the proper judicial authority any effort to impede their compliance with any law, any provision of this code, or any other official policy governing court interpreting and legal translating.

Canon 10: Professional Development

Interpreters shall continually improve their skills and knowledge and advance the profession through activities such as professional training and education, and interaction with colleagues and specialists in related fields.

National Association of Judiciary Interpreters and Translators (NAJIT)

Code of Ethics and Professional Responsibilities

As discussed in this manual, NAJIT is the national association that promotes the interests of court interpreters. The complete code and its commentary can be obtained at **http://najit.org**.

Canon 1: Accuracy

Source-language speech should be faithfully rendered into the target language by conserving all the elements of the original message while accommodating the syntactic and semantic patterns of the target language. The rendition should sound natural in the target language, and there should be no distortion of the original message through addition or omission, explanation or paraphrasing. All hedges, false starts and repetitions should be conveyed; also, English words mixed into the other language should be retained, as should culturally-bound terms which have no direct equivalent in English, or which may have more than one meaning. The register, style and tone of the source language should be conserved.

Guessing should be avoided. Court interpreters who do not hear or understand what a speaker has said should seek clarification. Interpreter errors should be corrected for the record as soon as possible.

Canon 2: Impartiality and Conflicts of Interest

Court interpreters and translators are to remain impartial and neutral in proceedings where they serve, and must maintain the appearance of impartiality and neutrality, avoiding unnecessary contact with the parties. Court interpreters and translators shall abstain from comment on matters in which they serve. Any real or potential conflict of interest shall be immediately disclosed to the Court and all parties as soon as the interpreter or translator becomes aware of such conflict of interest.

Canon 3: Confidentiality

Privileged or confidential information acquired in the course of interpreting or preparing a translation shall not be disclosed by the interpreter without authorization.

Canon 4: Limitations of Practice

Court interpreters and translators shall limit their participation in those matters in which they serve to interpreting and translating, and shall not give advice to the parties or otherwise engage in activities that can be construed as the practice of law.

Canon 5: Protocol and Demeanor

Court interpreters shall conduct themselves in a manner consistent with the standards and protocol of the court, and shall perform their duties as unobtrusively as possible. Court interpreters are to use the same grammatical person as the speaker. When it becomes necessary to assume a primary role in the communication, they must make it clear that they are speaking for themselves.

Canon 6: Maintenance and Improvement of Skills and Knowledge

Court interpreters and translators shall strive to maintain and improve their interpreting and translation skills and knowledge.

Canon 7: Accurate Representation of Credentials

Court interpreters and translators shall accurately represent their certifications, accreditations, training and pertinent experience.

Canon 8: Impediments to Compliance

Court interpreters and translators shall bring to the Court's attention any circumstance or condition that impedes full compliance with any Canon of this Code, including interpreter fatigue, in ability to hear, or inadequate knowledge of specialized terminology, and must decline assignments under conditions that make such compliance patently impossible.

Federal Court Interpreter Ethics and Protocol

Federally certified court interpreters, or any interpreters working in federal courts, are required to adhere to the following code of ethics. The code is available online at **http://sdnyinterpreters.org/pub/index.php?page=SDNYethics.html**.

Federal Court Interpreter Ethics and Protocol

1. Court interpreters, whether staff or freelance, serve the interest of the court. Their only function is to interpret accurately and faithfully, and with complete impartiality.

2. Court interpreters reflect proper court decorum and act with dignity and respect for court personnel, parties to the case, and the public.

3. Court interpreters shall not disclose any confidential information related to a case.

4. Court interpreters shall avoid unnecessary contact with witnesses, defendants and their families, and shall have no contact with jurors.

5. Court interpreters shall refrain from giving legal advice to any party or expressing personal opinion in a matter before the court.

6. Court interpreters must accurately state their professional qualifications and decline any assignment for which they are unprepared.

7. Interpreters have the duty to correct any material error in the interpretation of testimony. If anyone challenges an interpretation, they should objectively decide whether a correction should be made.

8. Court interpreters are forbidden from accepting any gift, gratuity or valuable consideration in excess of their authorized or contracted compensation.

I have read the above Code of Professional Responsibility and understand my ethical obligations when working in federal court or on any assignment related to a federal court case.

I hereby swear, affirm or promise that I shall accurately and faithfully interpret during any and all proceedings before the court to the best of my knowledge and ability.

Appendix 2

Resources for Self-Study

While most self-study resources target court inter-preting rather than non-courtroom legal interpreting, the terminology (and interpreting) practice they provide will still be of immense benefit to legal interpreters. It will also enhance their confidence and professionalism and help prepare for the certification test, if that is a goal of the interpreter.

Multilingual resources

ACEBO puts out many products for legal interpret-ers. *The Interpreter's Edge* by Holly Mikkelson is a famous resource for legal interpreters available in nine languages (Spanish, Cantonese, Mandarin, Korean, Vietnamese, Polish, Russian, Japanese, Portuguese), as well as a language-generic version. It consists of a book and a series of CDs or cassettes for practicing consecu-tive, simultaneous and sight translation modes. The book includes a bilingual legal glossary. However, this program also provides excellent practice for building legal terminology. While the focus is on court inter-preting, it will be useful for any legal interpreters.

- *The Interpreter's Edge, Spanish, 3rd edition*
- *The Interpreter's Edge,* Generic Edition (all languages)
- *The Interpreter's Edge,* Generic Edition *with CD sets in any of the other languages*
- *The Interpreter's Companion,* Fourth Edition
- *The Interpreter's Companion on CD-ROM*
- *Edge 21: An Interpreter's Edge for the 21st Century* (Spanish only):
    - Edge 21: Consecutive Interpreting
    - Edge 21: Simultaneous Interpreting
    - Edge 21: Sight Translation

There are additional self-study products available, particularly for Spanish interpreters. The cost varies according to the product. For more information, go to **www.acebo.com.**

LingvoSoft FlashCards 2008 offers a software program for English-Spanish and also for many other languages. Created as a vocabulary building activ-ity for language learners, it includes not only legal terminology but business, computer, medical, and three different levels of general vocabulary. For more information, go to **www.lingvosoft.com/Windows-Language-Learning-Software-items/.**

Spanish resources

The NCSC *Court Interpreter Practice Examina-tion Kit—Spanish.* The kit includes an instruction Manual, CD with audio files containing the practice exam and a passing performance on the examination, and hard copies of the test scripts. For more informa-tion go to **http://www.ncsconline.org/.**

Interpretapes, produced by the University of Ari-zona Agnes Haury Institute for Court Interpretation, are three sets of CDs designed to help aspiring court and legal interpreters enhance their interpreting skills. The only equipment necessary to successfully use INTERPRETAPES is a CD player with head-phones and an additional recording unit.

Federal Court Certification Practice Exam (Oral and Written)

The website for the NCSC Consortium on certifica-tion offers information about the Federal Court Interpreter Certification Exam (FCICE) as well as a Sample Written Examination for court interpreters and information about online practice oral testing. The practice test is available along with answer key as part of the Examine Handbook. This full-length practice examination for both the Written and Oral Examinations may help the interpreter concentrate on areas where additional study and practice is needed. There is no charge for obtaining the handbook online. The practice test is identical in structure to the FCICE. The Examinee Handbook also has suggestions for preparing for both the Written Examination and the Oral Examination, including reference materials. For information about the federal court certification program go to **http://www.ncsconline.org**. The handbook itself, including the practice exam, is available.

Distance learning resource

These short independent study courses are available on a variety of topics professional development for certified interpreters. Topics include "Discrimination," "Off the Record," "Psychological evaluations," "Anatomy of a Deposition," "Paralanguage/Body Language," "A Comparison of Criminal and Civil Law," "Sexual Harassment," "Elder Abuse," and others. The CDs/cassettes include answers and no computer is required. The CDs/cassettes cost $15 each. For more information, go to **http://aliciaernand.com/html/independent_study.html**.

Dictionaries and Glossaries

All legal interpreters need a good monolingual dictionary, a general bilingual dictionary and a bilingual legal dictionary, glossary or set of glossaries.

How Can I Find the Right Dictionary?

Solicit references from professional interpreters, where possible. Join the NAJIT listserv and post a question online, *e.g.*, how to find an English-Farsi legal dictionary. While the Internet is now an excellent resource for bilingual dictionaries, interpreters may also wish to consult a specialized bookstore such as Intrans Books:

Intrans Books (Formerly IBD)
P.O. Box 467
24 Hudson Street
Kinderhook, NY 12106
1-800-343-3531
www.ibdltd.com

Another bookshop is Schoenhof's Foreign Books, carrying a number of bilingual dictionaries, **www.schoenhofs.com,** or call 615-547-8855 to order a catalog.

One bookstore frequented by interpreters in or near Washington, D.C. is:

REITER'S Bookstore
1990 K St NW
Washington, DC 20006
202-223-3327
www.reiters.com
books@reiters.com

For what appears to be the longest listing of general and technical bilingual dictionaries for interpreters and translators available in print, consult Sofer, Morry (2004), *The Translator's Handbook*, 5th edition. Rockville, MD: Schreiber Publishing (**www.SchreiberLanguage.com**). The dictionaries listed there include a large number of European, Asian and African languages. This book also lists software resources for a number of languages. Language Marketplace, a translation and interpreter service based in Ontario, offers a website listing dozens of dictionaries that may be of use to interpreters, including some of the more challenging languages such as Swahili, Tamil, specific dialects of Arabic (such as Algerian and Egyptian), Bengal, Estonian, Icelandic, Indonesian and many others. For more information go to: **http://www.languagemarketplace.com/Translations_Services_Links.html#dictionaries**.

Interpreters may also wish to visit a website offered by a Nova Scotia interpreters association on interpreter dictionaries, at **http://www.atins.org/english/tools/dictionaries.shtml**. Pocket-sized electronic dictionary-translators are also available from several companies in a variety of languages, most costing between $100 and $500 (and up). Vocabulary may be limited to regular dictionary entries rather than specialized terminology. See below for examples. Interpreters can also conduct searches at **www.Amazon.com** and other online bookstores by plugging in keywords like "German legal" or "Albanian dictionary." (However, too many keywords may narrow the search down too far.)

Dictionary Software

The software dictionary industry has made many strides forward. Here are a few examples.

iFinger is a dictionary search engine which automatically attaches itself to the active window and gives immediate access to any reference content that purchasers choose to buy and download to their hard drive, including monolingual, bilingual and specialized dictionaries, such as legal (*e.g.*, for Spanish the *Diccionario Espasa Terminos Juridicos*). The user types up a term, and the definitions/references from all the dictionaries come up at the same time. The user can compare them. Languages include Dutch, English, Finnish, French, German, Italian, Norwegian and Spanish. The cost varies according to how many software dictionaries the user purchases. For example, the Spanish legal dictionary is about $44, while the large Spanish monolingual dictionary is $63, and the user probably would want a good English dictionary as well such as Merriam Webster ($39). For details go to **www.ifinger.com.**

Various hand-held electronic dictionaries are also popular. See, for example, **www.worldlanguage.com** or **www.ectaco.com.**

Dictionaries and Glossaries (print resources)

Monolingual (English) dictionaries

American Heritage Dictionaries (2006). *The American Heritage Dictionary of the English Language*, 4th ed. Houghton Mifflin, 2112 pp.

Merriam-Webster (2000). *Webster's Third New International Dictionary, Unabridged, Book and CD-ROM Dictionary of the English Language.* Merriam-Webster. 2783 pp.

Bryan A. Garner (2004). *Black's Law Dictionary*, 8th ed. West. 1323 pp. A comprehensive reference work.

Steven H. Gifis (2003). *Barron's Law Dictionary*, 5th ed. Barron's Educational Series. 608 pp. This dictionary is for law students. It is small, light-weight, inexpensive and has simple explanations that are easier to understand than the more comprehensive Black's Law Dictionary.

William C. Burton (1999). *Burton's Legal Thesaurus.* Wiley. 1012 pp.

Spanish/English Dictionaries for judiciary interpreters

Butterworths Legal Publishers English/Spanish Legal Dictionary. Diccionario Jurídico Ingles/Español by Guillermo Cabanellas de las Cuevas and Eleanor C. Hoague (2 vol. set)

Bilingual Dictionary of Criminal Justice Terms (English/Spanish) by Virginia Benmaman, Norma C. Connolly, Scott Robert Loos Gould Publications.

Bilingual Dictionary of Immigration Terms Norma C. Connolly Gould Publications Phone (407) 695-9500 ISBN 0-87526-541-3

Bilingual Dictionary of Domestic Relations and Juvenile Terms Norma C. Connolly Gould Publications Phone (407) 695-9500 ISBN 0-87526-540-5

Barron's Spanish Idioms ISBN 0-8120-9027-6. Simon and Schuster's International Dictionary, Eng./Span., Span./Eng., Simon and Schuster, Inc., Prentice Hall, NY

Criminal Court Dictionary (English/Spanish) by Dennis McKenna. Updated in 2009.

A comprehensive monolingual dictionary:

Diccionario de la Lengua Española

Diccionario de Uso del Español (2 volumes)

General bilingual dictionaries:

Larousse Gran Diccionario Español-Ingles/Ingles-Español

Simon and Schuster International Dictionary English-Spanish/Spanish-English

Unabridged Spanish Dictionary, Harper Collins

Legal dictionaries

Guillermo Cabanellas de las Cuevas and Eleanor C. Hoague (1998), *Dictionario Juridico Espanol-Ingles.* Editorial Heliasta

Terminos Juridicos Ingles-Espanol Spanish-English (1995), 688 pp.

Bilingual Dictionary of Criminal Justice Terms (English-Spanish)

The following general and specialized dictionaries in various languages other than English and Spanish can be looked up on the Internet to order online or through a reputable bookseller specialized in dictionaries (see above).

Arabic

Al Mawrid (1998) English-Arabic/Arabic-English dictionary

Al Mawrid (2002): A Modern English-Arabic Dictionary

Arabic-English Faruqi's Law Dictionary (also available in English-Arabic)

Chinese

Chinese-English Dictionary (1991), 1401 pp.

English-Chinese Dictionary (1991), 1769 pp.

Chinese-English New Practical Dictionary (1987) 1418 pp.

Chinese-English (Mandarin) Dictionary (1967), 660 pp.

English-Chinese Glossary of American Criminal Law (1989), 246 pp.

Glossary of Selected Legal Terms English-Cantonese: Office of the Administrator of the Courts, State of Washington. Distributed by ACEBO, P.O. Box 7485, CA 93962

French

Dictionnaire Encyclopedique, 2 vols (1994), 2124 pp.

Le Nouveau Petit Robert: Dictionnaire De La Langue Française (2002)

Harper Collins Robert French Unabridged Dictionary (2002, 6th ed) 2142 pp.

English-French Lexicon of Legal Terms S:\RTS\ Interpretation\Interp-consortium\Web\Web site redesign\Web 4 Essential Dictionaries.doc

Haitian Creole

Haitian Creole-English-French Dictionary Deslan Rincher & Associates 22-11 Church Ave Brooklyn, NY 11226 (718) 693-0461

Haitian Creole-English-French Dictionary (1981) Bloomington Indiana-Creole Institute Haitiana Publications 170-08 Hillside Ave. Jamaica, NY 11432 (718) 523-0135

Haitian Creole-English Dictionary Targetej, Dunwoody Press A legal bilingual dictionary

Italian

Italian Encyclopedia Universal Dictionary (1860 pp.)

Italian-English English-Italian Dictionary (*Sansoni*)

English-Italian Law Dictionary (1994)

Italian-English Law Dictionary (1996)

Korean

Korean-English Dictionary (1994), 2182 pp., Publisher: Minjungseorim

English-Korean Dictionary (1994), 2687 pp., Publisher: Minjung

English-Korean Glossary (**www.acebo.com**)

Polish

The Great Polish/English Dictionary (1992) 2 Volume set, 1728 pp.

The Great English/Polish Dictionary (1992), 1404 pp.

Format: Hardcover; 1404 pp.

Polish/English Dictionary of Legal Terms

English/Polish Dictionary of Legal and Economic Terms (1991), 724 pp.

Portuguese

Portuguese Dictionary-Novo

Pequeno Dicionário Enciclopédico Koogan Larousse

> Editoria Larousse do Brasil, Rio de Janeiro
> Imported Books. P.O. Box 4414 Dallas Texas
> (214) 941-6497

Dictionary Portuguese-English, 2 volumes, 1328 pp.

English-Portuguese Dictionary, 1151 pp.

Legal bilingual dictionaries:

Dicionário Jurídico, 3rd ed. 1987, a legal
bilingual dictionary

Maria Chaves de Mello. Rio de Janeiro: Barristers's
Editors

Noronha's Legal Dictionary (1993)

Durval de Noronha Goyos, Jr.

Sao Paulo: Editora Observador Legal (1993)

Russian

Russian Encyclopedic Dictionary, 1632 pp.

English-Russian Dictionary (1988, 2 Volumes)
2108 pp.

Russian-English Translator's Dictionary (1991),
735 pp.

Russian-English Legal Dictionary

English-Russian Dictionary of American Criminal Law

> Available from Greenwood Publishing Group
> P.O. Box 5007, Westport, CT 06881-5007

Vietnamese

Vietnamese-English/English-Vietnamese Dictionary
(1992), 826 pp.

A legal bilingual dictionary: *English-Vietnamese
Glossary* (**www.acebo.com**)

Legal Glossaries

Print legal glossaries in five Asian languages—
Cantonese, Korean, Vietnamese, Khmer, and
Laotian—are available from a well-known company
called Acebo. Each glossary contains translations of
approximately 450 of the most widely used English

legal terms. These glossaries were developed by certified, working court interpreters under the direction
of the Washington State Office of the Administrator
for the Courts and the State Justice Institute of
Alexandria, Virginia. Glossaries are loose leaf and
three-hole drilled for insertion into your own binder.
The cost is $5 each plus shipping. For more informa-
tion, go to **http://acebo.com/asian.htm.**

Online Legal Dictionaries and Glossaries

English

English Legal Glossary. National Consortium of State
Courts, 49 pp. **http://www.ncsconline.org/wc/
publications/Res_CtInte_EnglishLegalGlossary
Pub.pdf**

Glossary of Selected Terms. For juvenile cases. Ten-
nessee Administrative Office of the Courts, 9 pp.
**http://www.tsc.state.tn.us/geninfo/Publications/
Forms/Interpreters/Juvenileglosss.pdf**

Street Terms: Drugs and the Drug Trade. Executive
Office of the President, Office of Drug Control
Policy, 38 pp. **http://www.streetdrugs.org/pdf/
street_terms.pdf**

Immigration: for a glossary of immigration terms
by the U.S. Citizenship and Immigration Services,
go to **www.uscis.gov** click on Education &
Resources, then Glossary (immigration terms). For
another glossary of immigration terms put out by
an organization called Immigration Equality, go to:
www.immigrationequality.org.

General legal glossaries:

http://www.lectlaw.com/def.htm. (clear definitions)

http://dictionary.law.com/ (short and long
definitions)

http://www.nolo.com/definition.cfm/alpha/A, or
http://www.nolo.com/glossary.cfm

http://www.mylawyer.com/glossary.htm

http://www.nycourthelp.gov/TermsGlossary.html

http://www.nwjustice.org/glossary/index.html

Spanish

The Language of Justice. A Spanish Glossary for New York City. The Vera Institute. 50 pp. http://www.vera.org/publication_pdf/395_774.pdf.

English-Spanish Legal Glossary. Superior Court of California, County of Sacramento. 212 pp. http://www.saccourt.com/geninfo/legal_glossaries/glossaries/English%20Spanish%20Legal%20Glossary%20Rev%200806.pdf

Centro de Ayuda de las cortes de California: http://www.courtinfo.ca.gov/selfhelp/espanol/glosario.htm

Glossary of Legal (and Related) Terms and Courthouse Signs. English/Spanish. New Jersey Administrative Office of the Courts. 19 pp. http://www.judiciary.state.nj.us/interpreters/glossary2.pdf

Free Glossary/dictionary of English/Spanish Court Terms, 161 pages, compiled by Ernesto Romero: http://www.ernestoromero.net/LS.pdf

Spanish-English Glossary. The United States District Court, Southern District of New York. http://www.sdnyinterpreters.org/glossary.php

In addition to the ability to type in a word in English and ask for the translation into Spanish, there is a drop-down menu called "Categories." Click on subjects like "attorney-client interviews," "legal," "idioms," etc. This glossary was created by SDNY interpreters. It is a work in progress but has many terms. The search box can be set to English or Spanish.

The NCSC Spanish examination practice kit dictionaries/test items (these are free): http://www.ncsconline.org/D_Research/CIPEK_Dictionaries.html

Chinese

Translating Justice: A Traditional Chinese Glossary for New York City. The Vera Institute. 50 pp. http://www.vera.org/publication_pdf/396_775.pdf

Hmong

Hmong Legal Glossary. Wisconsin Court System, 74 pp. http://www.wicourts.gov/services/interpreter/docs/hmongglossary.pdf

French

Dictionnaire d'anglais économique et juridique. http://www.inventerm.com/Resultat.aspx

This resource is put out by Quebec Office de la langue française. The interpreter can perform a search *e.g.,* for "legal" and come up with 976 terms (in March 2008) with a French-French glossary.

Arabic

English-Arabic Legal Glossary. Superior Court of California, County of Sacramento, 105 pp. http://www.saccourt.com/geninfo/legal_glossaries/glossaries/Arabic_English_Legal_Glossary.pdf

Russian

California http://www.saccourt.ca.gov/general/legal-glossaries/docs/russian-legal-glossary.pdf

Multilingual

For bilingual, online legal glossaries from the Superior Court of California in Arabic, Armenian, Mien, Mong, Punjabi, Romanian, Russian, Spanish and Vietnamese, go to http://www.saccourt.ca.gov/general/legal-glossaries/docs/russian-legal-glossary.pdf

Multilingual Legal Glossary. Vancouver Community College. http://www.legalglossary.ca/dictionary/ This is a search-by-term online glossary of 5,000 Canadian legal and court-related terms in English Plain Language. These terms are available in Chinese (Simplified), Chinese (Traditional), Farsi, Punjabi, Russian, Spanish and Vietnamese. For more information about how the glossary works, see http://legalglossary.ca/dictionary/about.asp.

For Chinese, Korean, Spanish and Vietnamese, go to the California Courts Self Help Center at http://www.courtinfo.ca.gov/selfhelp/languages/.

For Danish, Dutch, Finnish, French, German, Italian, Norwegian, Portuguese, Spanish and Swedish, see the Europa Glossary at http://europa.eu/scadplus/glossary/index_A_es.htm (offers both general and legal terminology).

Online General Dictionaries (English)

Multilingual

- www.wordreference.com is a valuable, user-friendly online dictionary. Select the two languages, type in the word for which a translation is desired in one language, and the translation of that word (and other information) appears instantly.

- **http://www.freedict.com** offers links to bidirectional dictionaries in 16 languages.
- **www.your Dictionary.com**
- **http://www.lexicool.com/**
- Lexicool.com's online dictionary search engine currently has links to over 3500 bilingual and multilingual dictionaries and glossaries.
- **http://www.logos.it/pls/dictionary/linguistic_resources.main?lang=en&source=resources** 1,016 glossaries in over 60 languages

Online General Dictionaries in Specific Languages

Chinese

http://zhongwen.com/zi.htm

English

http://www.uiuc.edu/cgi-bin/oed (Oxford English Dictionary)
http://humanities.uchicago.edu/forms_unrest/ROGET.html (Roget's Thesaurus)

Hindi

http://www3.aa.tufs.ac.jp/~kmach/hnd_la-e.htm#wordanalysis (no verbs)
http://www3.aa.tufs.ac.jp/~kmach/hnd_la-e.htm#wordanalysis (verbs)

Japanese

http://www.freedict.com/onldict/jap.html

Khmer

http://www.ximplex.com/khmer/dicts/ek.asp

Korean

http://www.human.toyogakuen-u.ac.jp/~acmuller/cjkdict.htm

Russian

http://www.angelfire.com/vt/kuzy/dictionary.html (links to English-Russian and Russian-English dictionaries) http://www.freedict.com/onldict/rus.html

Serbian

http://129.97.74.78/cgi-bin/cgiwrap/vkeselj/r2cnik.pl, http://www.grad.math.uwaterloo.ca/%7Evkeselj/#contact

Spanish

http://www.vox.es
http://www.freedict.com/onldict/spa.html

Swahili

http://www.yale.edu/swahili/
http://www.freedict.com/onldict/swa.html

Tagalog

http://www.foreignword.com

Urdu

http://host.bip.net/tracker/dict/index.html/ (English-Urdu only)

Vietnamese

http://www.saigon.com/~vietdict/index.html

International Book Distributers

For all languages:

Imported books

2025 West Clarendon
P.O. Box 4414
Dallas, TX 75208
(214) 941-6497

i.b.d., Ltd.

International Book Distributors
24 Hudson St
Kinderhook, NY 12106
(800) 343-3531

Schoenhof's Foreign Books
76A Mount Auburn Street
Cambridge, MA 02138
(617) 547-8855

United Nations Bookstore
G.A. 32 New York, NY 10017
(212) 963-7680

Spanish books

Ediciones Universal
P.O. Box 450353
Miami, FL 33245-0353
(305) 642-3234

Appendix 3

Training Programs for Legal Interpreters

James Madison University (JMU), Harrisonburg, Virginia

Center for Translation and Interpretation
Minors and certificates in translation and localization
http://www.jmu.edu/forlang/trans

Kent State University: http://appling.kent.edu

Monterey Institute of International Studies
Graduate School of Translation and Interpretation
http://www.miis.edu/gsti-about-dean.html

New York University School of Continuing and Professional Studies
http://www.nyu.edu

University of Arizona
The National Center for Interpretation Testing, Research and Policy
http://w3.arizona.edu/~ncitrp

University of Charleston, South Carolina
Graduate Program in Bilingual Legal Interpreting
http://www.cofc.edu/~legalist

University of North Carolina at Charlotte
http://www.uncc.edu/langweb/Sp/index.htm
http://www.uncc.edu/langweb/sp/MA/index.htm

Professional Organizations

National Association of Judiciary Interpreters and Translators (NAJIT): www.najit.org

American Translators Association (ATA):
www.atanet.org

National Capital Area Chapter of the ATA
(NCATA): www.ncata.org

For other chapters of the ATA across the U.S., go to:
http://www.atanet.org/chaptersandgroups/chapters.php

For groups affiliated with the ATA, go to:
http://www.atanet.org/chaptersandgroups/affiliated_groups.php

For a listing of other groups that support interpreters and translators, go to:

http://www.atanet.org/chaptersandgroups/other_groups.php

National Center for State Courts (NCSC):
www.ncsconline.org

Court and Community Interpreters of Ohio:
www.ccio.org

Bibliographies on Interpreting

A Bibliography on Court and Legal Interpreting
by Ruth Morris
http://aiic.net/ViewPage.cfm/article146

Critical Link resources
http://www.criticallink.org/English/linksresources.htm
Critical Link provides links to bibliographies concerning such topics as legal, medical and community interpreting.

Bibliography on Interpreting and Translation (BITRA); Universidad de Alicante
http://cv1.cpd.ua.es/tra_int/usu/buscar.asp?idioma=en
This site provides a searchable database of interpreting and translation materials.

"

Government Resources

National Center for State Courts

This organization offers a wealth of information and publications on legal interpreting from across the country. It also gives information on which states are now part of the consortium of courts that certifies interpreters in several languages and offers them orientation and training.

http://www.ncsconline.org/

Court Interpreter Practice Examination Kit –The Spanish version of this kit is available at: **http://www. ncsconline.org/D_Research/CIPEK.html**

"Access to Justice: Protection Orders and Limited English Proficiency."

This free NCSC DVD is a training tool designed both for court staff who may have to assist petitioners with limited English proficiency and as a resource for domestic violence advocates who interpret for clients. To receive a free copy, write to **cgreen@ncsc. dni.us.**

State Court Rules for Language Interpreters
http://www.ncsc.dni.us/is/MEMOS/S99-1242.htm

Department of Justice Final LEP Guidance Federal Register: June 18, 2002 **www.lep.gov** Click on "Federal Agencies"

Breaking Down the Language Barrier Translating Limited English Proficiency into Practice (Training Video) **www.lep.gov** Click on "Federal Agencies"

Letter from U.S. Department of Justice **www. languageaccess.us** Click on "Resources"

Executive Order 13166 Limited English Proficiency Resource Document: Tip and Tools from the Field. **http://lep.gov/tips_tools_92104.htm**

Language Identification "I Speak Cards" by the Ohio Office of Criminal Justice Services **www.languageaccess.us** Click on "resources" page two

Interagency Language Roundtable **http://www. govtilr.org/**

Interpreters FAQ
http://www.nysd.uscourts.gov/interp.htm

Books and Articles

Fundamentals of Court Interpretation: Theory, Policy and Practice by Roseann Dueñas González, Victoria F. Vasquez, Holly Mikkelson (Carolina Academic Press (919) 489-7486)

The Bilingual Courtroom: Court Interpreters in the Judicial Process by Susan Berk-Seligson
ISBN 0-226-04373-8

NAJIT position papers, advocacy letters and general articles on legal interpreting at: **www.najit.org** Click on NAJIT Advocacy

NAJIT's index of articles that have appeared in the U.S. press about interpreter-related issues between 2003 and 2007. While not exhaustive, the index provides a summary of the article content and the bibliographic reference so that a researcher may locate the original. Click on Publications and then click on Searchable index of interpreter-related articles in the news.

Getting it Right by Doing it Right by Isabel Framer **www.languageaccess.us** Click on "resources"

"Translation Getting It Right" A guide to buying translations
http://www.atanet.org/docs/Getting_it_right.pdf

Interpreter Issues on Appeals by Dr. Virginia Benmaman **www.najit.org.** Click on Publications and then click on "Proteus"

Interpreters and Their Impact on the Criminal Justice System; The Alejandro Ramirez Story, by Isabel Framer **www.languageaccess.us.** Click on "resources"

Through the Eyes of an Interpreter by Isabel Framer **www.languageaccess.us.** Click on "resources"

Explanation of Certification by Isabel Framer **www.languageaccess.us.**Click on "resources"

Interpreting The Interpreter: What Every LAV Attorney And Advocate Needs To Know About Legal Interpretation by Isabel Framer. **www.languageaccess.us.** Click on "resources"

National Association for Judiciary Interpreters and Translators

This professional association supports legal interpreters across the country and provides a wealth of resources, including a code of ethics, a quarterly newsletter called *Proteus,* glossaries, manuals, and other publications. NAJIT also offers workshops and seminars for training and continuing education and sponsors presentations at national meetings of other interpreters and translators associations and related professions. **www.najit.org**

Society for the Study of Translation and Interpretation

This 501(c)(3) nonprofit arm of NAJIT offers testing, test preparation workshops and training to support legal interpreters, especially those seeking to become court certified. For details see the NAJIT website at **www.najit.org.**

Resources on Law

Cornell Legal Information Institute

One of the first Legal Research sites on the Internet, Cornell Law School's Legal Information Institute has an extremely large collection of law-related resources and links. The site includes links to case law, statutes and regulations at both the federal and state levels. **www.law.cornell.com**

Law in a Nutshell series from West Group

These books cover various areas of law should be available at local law school libraries and book stores as well as on-line. They are written in real English and give a history of the issue and then an overview.

Immigration Law and Procedure: Desk Edition

Stanley Mailman, Esq., Satterlee, Stephens, Burke & Burke, LLP, Daniel M. Kowalski. Published by Matthew Bender and updated twice yearly, this is a compact version of the 20-volume "bible" of immigration law.

Findlaw

Findlaw (**www.findlaw.com**) provides an impressive collection of case law and boasts free access to US Supreme Court decisions dating back to 1893. The site's news page tracks recent legal news on a wide array of topics (**http://legalnews.findlaw.com/**). Some interpreters like to look up cases at www.findlaw.com/casecode; the service is available at no charge and some interpreters find it easier to look up case law on Findlaw than Lexis-Nexis (a paid service).

Findlaw's Health Law topic page at **http://www. findlaw.com/01topics/19health/index.html** offers dozens of links to useful health law resources on the Internet.

Hieros Gamos

According to this website, "Hieros Gamos" means the harmonization of seeming opposites. The "opposites" that this website seeks to harmonize are electronic and written information. To do this, the creators of this website have amassed an index of over 100,000 web pages dealing with law and government, which can be accessed via either keyword search or browsing by topic. **www.hg.org**

The Internet Law Library

This site was discontinued on May 28, 1999. Originally developed by the US House of Representatives in 1994, it included the US Code, other federal laws, state and territorial laws, as well as treaties and international law. The US Code was transferred to the Office of the Law Revision Counsel (**http://uscode. house.gov/**), while the rest of the collection was made available to other sites. **http//law.house.gov**

The Virtual Chase

This site was created by a law librarian with extensive experience in online research. The site contains links to hundreds of legal research resources on the Internet. The site's Annotated Guide to Resources for Legal Professionals is particularly useful. **www.virtrualchase.com**

The Health Law Resource

The focus of the website is on provider transactions and legislation affecting health care. Topic pages on this website include privacy, Medicare/Medicaid, and fraud & abuse. **www.netreach.net**

National Health Law Program (NHeLP)

A national nonprofit organization, NHeLP offers many excellent resources and publications for interpreters on legal issues related to health care. Go to **www.healthlaw.org.**

Government Printing Office

The Government Printing Office website provides access to a wide array of federal government documents, including the Code of Federal Regulations, the Federal Register, and Government Accounting Office (GAO) reports. This very large database of federal documents is also available via the Federal Depository Library Gateways, a list of which can be accessed at

www.access.gpo.gov/su_docs/aces/aaces004.html

Special Resource

Cambridge University "International Legal English" website

**http://cdextras.cambridge.org/VocabTrainer/
intlegalenglish/**

This website includes terminology study activities; exercises; and games. Legal terminology is divided into sectors. A rich and fascinating resource.

Appendix 4

In 1974, Congress enacted the creation of the Legal Services Corporation (LSC) to fund legal aid services across the country. The intent is to promote equal access to justice for low-income residents.

The LEP guidance of the Legal Services Corporation (LSC) specifies the steps that grantees should in order to be prepared to effectively serve LEP individuals in need of legal assistance. The complete document is available at **http://www.lsc.gov/ program/pl/pl2004-2LEPGuidance.pdf**.

The guidance advises agencies as follows: (The points below are summarized briefly by the authors, with emphasis added. See the complete guidance for details.)

- Conduct a needs assessment.
- Develop a program policy that reflects needs and resources.
- Determine when an individual has LEP, including the **preferred language** of the individual and the need for an interpreter.
- Recruit and hire bilingual staff for major language groups in the program's service area.
- **Train [bilingual] staff to interpret.**
- Obtain *competent* **interpretation services** for each of the major languages in the program's service area.
- **Regularly train all staff who interact with LEP individuals** on how best to access language services, on how to respond appropriately to LEP individuals and on how **best to use bilingual staff and interpreters.**
- Plan to translate all vital program documents into languages of the target LEP communities in the program's service area.
- Strategize the dissemination of information about the availability of bilingual staff or free interpreters and revise and translate outreach materials.

While not all LSC agencies have successfully implemented these model policies, progress is being made across the nation and awareness of the proper use of interpreters and translators is growing. Since 2006, LSC has begun making efforts to review the compliance of grantees with the LEP guidance.

The guidance includes a strong recommendation to use a variety of interpreter resources (bilingual staff or bilingual volunteers trained to interpret, contract interpreters and telephonic interpreters). The guidance also *strongly discourages the use of family and friends* as interpreters. It essentially prohibits the use of minor children to interpret except in emergencies.

Selected Bibliography

ACEBO (1998, 2006 a). *Consecutive Interpreting Theory and Consecutive Note-taking.* DVD (2006) and accompanying manual (1998) produced by ACEBO (www.acebo.com) and narrated by Holly Mikkelson.

ACEBO (1998, 2006 b). *The Interpreter's Code of Ethics & The Role of the Interpreter in the Courtroom.* DVD (2006) and accompanying manual (1998) produced by ACEBO (www.acebo.com) and narrated by Holly Mikkelson.

Ahmad, Muneer I. (2007). Interpreting Communities: Lawyering Across Language Difference. *UCLA Law Review,* 54:999-1086.

Baker, Mona (1998). *Routledge Encyclopedia of Translation Studies.* London: Routeledge.

Berk-Seligson, Susan (2002). *The Bilingual Courtroom: Court Interpreters in the Judicial Process.* Chicago: University of Chicago Press.

California Healthcare Interpreting Association (2000). *California Standards for Healthcare Interpreters.* Sacramento, CA: CHIA. Available at www.chiaonling.org.

Davis, J. (1980). Transcripts of *U.S. v. Hanigan,* No. CR-79-2060-RMB. Quoted in González *et al*: 605). Available from Official Court Reporter, United States District Court, P.O. Box 142, Tucson, 5702.

Diriker, Ebru (2004). *De-/Re-Contextualizing Conference Interpreting: Interpreters in the Ivory Tower?* Series: Benjamins Translation Library, 53. Amsterdam/Philadelphia: John Benjamins.

Garber, Nathan (2000) Community interpretation: A personal view. In Roberts, Roda P., Carr, Silvana E., Abraham, Diana, Dufour, Aideen (Eds), *Critical Link 2: Interpreters in the Community. Selected Papers Proceedings* from the Second International Conference on Interpreting in Legal, Health, and Social Service. Herndon, VA: John Benjamin pp 9-20.

González, Roseann Dueñas, Vasquez, Victoria F., Mikkelson, Holly (1991) *Fundamentals of Court Interpretation,* Durham, North Carolina: Carolina Academic Press.

Healthcare Interpretation Network (2007). *National Standard Guide for Community Interpreting Services.* Toronto: Healthcare Interpretation Network. Available at http:// healthcareinterpretation.homestead.com/National_Standard_ Guide_for_Community_Interpreting_Services.pdf.

Houseman, Alan W. and Perle, Linda E (2007). *A Brief History of Civil Legal Assistance in the United States.* Washington, DC: Center for Law and Social Policy, 2003, revised in 2007.

Ieracci, Vanessa (2003) NAJIT's 25th year: Past, present and future. *Proteus,* 13:3. http://najit.org/members_only/proteus/v13n3/ Vol13_No3_Ieraci.PDF, February 13, 2008.

Legal Services Corporation (2004). Guidance to LSC Programs for Serving Client Eligible Individuals with Limited English Proficiency. Washington, DC: LSC. Available at http://www.lri.lsc. gov/pdfs/05071801.pdf.

Mazza, Cristina (2001). Numbers in simultaneous interpretation. *The Interpreters' Newsletter*, 11. Available at http://hdl.handle. net/10077/2450.

Mikkelson, Holly (1998). Towards a redefinition of the role of the court interpreter. *Interpreting.* 3.1:21-45

Moeketsi, R.H. (2003). Redefining the role of the South African court interpreter. *Proteus 8 (3-4).* http://www.najit. org/members_only/proteus/v8n3-4/moekesti_v8n3-4.htm

Morris, Ruth (1995). The Moral dilemmas of court interpreting. *The Translator* Volume 1, Number 1 (1995) 25-46.

National Association of Judiciary Interpreters and Translators (2005) *NAJIT Position Paper: Summary Interpreting in Legal Settings.* Seattle, WA. Available at www.najit.org.

National Council on Interpreting in Health Care (2004). *A National Code of Ethics for Interpreters in Health Care.* Washington, DC: NCIHC. Available at http://data.memberclicks.com/site/ ncihc/NCIHC%20National%20Code%20of%20Ethics.pdf.

National Council on Interpreting in Health Care (2005). *National Standards of Practice for Interpreters in Health Care.* Washington, DC: NCIHC. Available at http://data.memberclicks.com/ site/ncihc/NCIHC%20National%20Standards%20of%20 Practice.pdf.

Pöchhacker, Franz (2001). Quality assessment in conference and community interpreting. *Meta* 46(2): 410-425.

Roat, Cynthia (1999). *Bridging the Gap: A Basic Training for Medical Interpreters*, 3rd Edition. Seattle: Cross Cultural Health Care Program.

Stewart, Bethan (2008). Language barrier can hinder the legal process. *The Idaho Statesman,* July 8, 2008.

Stytler, N.C. 1993. Implementing language rights in court: The role of the court interpreter in South Africa. The SA Journal on Human Rights. 9.2:205-222. In K. Prinsloo *et al* (eds) *Language, Law and Equality.* Pretoria: UNISA, 38-56.

Uekert, Brenda K., Peters, Tracy, Romberger, Wanda, Abraham, Margaret and Keilitz, Susan (2006). *Serving Limited English Proficient (LEP) Battered Women: A National Survey of the Courts' Capacity to Provide Protection Orders.* Arlington, VA: National Center for State Courts.

Viaggio, Sergio (2006) *A General Theory of Interlingual Interpretation.* London: Verlag für Wissenschaftliche Literatur.

Vidal, Mirta (1997). New study on fatigue confirms need for working in teams. *Proteus,* 6(1). Available at www.erudit.org/ revue/meta/2001/v46/n2/003847ar.pdf, access 3/11/08.

Legal Interpreting:
A Glossary *of* General Terms

This glossary is abstracted, with permission, from the National Center for State Courts Glossary of Commonly Used Court & Justice System Terminology, Feb. 8, 2001 version.

ACCUSATION – A formal charge against a person, to the effect that he has engaged in a punishable offense.

ACCUSED – The generic name for the defendant in a criminal case.

ACQUIT – To legally certify the innocence of one charged with a crime. To set free, release or discharge from an obligation, burden or accusation. To find a defendant not guilty in a criminal trial.

ACTION – Case, cause, suit, or controversy disputed or contested before a court of justice.

ADJUDICATE – To determine finally.

ADJUDICATION – Giving or pronouncing a judg-ment or decree. Also the judgment given.

ADMISSIBLE EVIDENCE – Evidence that can be legally and properly introduced in a civil or criminal trial.

ADMISSION – Voluntary acknowledgment of the existence of certain facts relevant to the adversary's case.

ADMONISH – To advise or caution. For example the Court may caution or admonish counsel for wrong practices.

ADOPTION – To take into one's family the child of another and give him or her the rights, privileges, and duties of a child and heir.

ADVERSARY SYSTEM – The trial method used in the U.S. and some other countries. This system is based on the belief that truth can best be determined by giving opposing parties full opportunity to present and establish their evidence, and to test by cross-examination the evidence presented by their adversaries. All this is done under the established rules of procedure before an impartial judge and/or jury.

AFFIDAVIT – A written statement of facts confirmed by the oath of the party making it, before a notary or officer having authority to administer oaths. For example, in criminal cases, affidavits are often used by police officers seeking to convince courts to grant a warrant to make an arrest or a search. In civil cases, affidavits of witnesses are often used to support motions for summary judgment.

AFFIRMED – In the practice of appellate courts, the word means that the decision of the trial court is correct.

AGENT – One who has authority to act for another.

AGGRAVATED ASSAULT – An attempt to cause serious bodily injury to another or purposely, knowingly or recklessly causing such injury, or an attempt to cause or purposely or knowingly cause bodily injury to another with a deadly weapon.

AGGRAVATED BATTERY – The unlawful use of force against another with unusual or serious consequences such as the use of a dangerous weapon.

AGGRAVATING FACTORS – Any factors associated with the commission of a crime which increase the seriousness of the offense or add to its injurious consequences.

AGREEMENT – A mutual understanding and intention between two or more parties. The writing or instrument which is evidence of an agreement. (Although often used as synonymous with contract, agreement is a broader term.)

ALIMONY – A court-ordered allowance that one spouse pays the other spouse for maintenance and support while they are either separated, pending suit for divorce, or after they are divorced.

ALLEGATION – The assertion of a party to an action, setting out what he expects to prove.

ALLEGE – To state, recite, assert, claim, maintain, charge or set forth. To make an allegation.

ALLEGED – Asserted to be true as depicted or a person who is accused but has not yet been tried in court.

ALTERNATIVE DISPUTE RESOLUTION (ADR) – Settling a dispute without a full, formal trial. Methods include *mediation, conciliation, arbitration, and settlement*, among others.

AMEND – To change, correct, revise, improve, modify, or alter.

AMENDMENT – The correction of an error admitted in any process.

ANSWER – The defendant's response to the plaintiff's allegations as stated in a complaint. An item-by-item, paragraph-by-paragraph response to points made in a complaint; part of the pleadings.

APPEAL – A request made after a trial, asking another court (usually the court of appeals) to decide whether the trial was conducted properly. To make such a request is "to appeal" or "to take an appeal."

APPEARANCE – A coming into court as party or interested person or as a lawyer on behalf of party or interested person.

APPELLANT – The party appealing a final decision or judgment.

APPELLATE COURT – A court having jurisdiction to hear appeals and review a trial court's procedure.

ARBITRATION – The referral of a dispute to an impartial third person chosen by the parties to the dispute who agree in advance to abide by the arbitrator's award issued after a hearing at which both parties have an opportunity to be heard.

ARGUMENT – Remarks addressed by attorney to judge or jury on the merits of case or on points of law.

ARREST – To deprive a person of his liberty by legal authority.

ARSON – The malicious burning of someone else's or one's own dwelling or of anyone's commercial or industrial property.

ASSAULT – Any willful attempt or threat to inflict injury upon the person of another, when coupled with the present ability to do so, and any intentional display of force such as would give victim reason to fear or expect immediate bodily harm.

ASSAULT WITH A DEADLY WEAPON – An aggravated unlawful assault in which there is threat to do bodily harm without justification or excuse by use of any instrument calculated to do serious bodily harm or cause death.

ASSAULT, AGGRAVATED – An assault committed with the intention of committing some additional crime.

ATTEMPT – An endeavor or effort to do an act or accomplish a crime, carries beyond preparation, but lacking execution.

ATTEST – To bear witness to, to affirm to be true or genuine, to certify.

ATTORNEY – Attorney at law, lawyer, counselor at law.

ATTORNEY OF RECORD – The lawyer who represents a client and is entitled to receive all formal documents from the court or from other parties. Also known as counsel of record.

AUTHENTICATE – To give authority or legal authenticity to a statute, record, or other written instrument.

BAIL – Money or other security (such as a bail bond) provided to the court to temporarily allow a person's release from jail and assure his or her appearance in court. *Bail* and *Bond* are often used interchangeably.

BAILIFF – A court officer who has charge of a court session in the matter of keeping order and has custody of the jury.

BANKRUPT – The state or condition of a person who is unable to pay his or her debts as they are or become due.

BANKRUPTCY – Refers to statutes and judicial proceedings involving persons or businesses that cannot pay their debts and seek the assistance of the court in getting a fresh start. Under the protection of the bankruptcy court, debtors may be released from or "discharged" from their debts, perhaps by paying a portion of each debt. Bankruptcy judges preside over these proceedings. The person with the debts is called the debtor and the people or companies to whom the debtor owes money to are called creditors.

BAR – 1. Historically, the partition separating the general public from the space occupied by the judges, lawyers, and other participants in a trial. 2. More commonly, the term means the whole body of lawyers.

BATTERED CHILD SYNDROME (B.C.S.) – Physical condition of a child indicating that external or internal injuries result from acts committed by a parent or custodian.

BATTERY – An offensive touching or use of force on a person without the person's consent.

BATTERY, SPOUSAL – An offensive touching or use of force on one's spouse without the spouse's consent. See BATTERY.

BENCH – The seat occupied by judges in courts.

BENCH CONFERENCE – A meeting either on or off the record at the judge's bench between the judge, counsel, and sometimes the defendant, out of the hearing of the jury.

BENCH TRIAL – Trial without a jury in which a judge decides the facts.

BENCH WARRANT – An order issued by a judge for the arrest of a person.

BENEFICIARY – Someone named to receive property or benefits in a will. In a trust, a person who is to receive benefits from the trust.

BEQUEATH – To give a gift to someone through a will.

BEQUESTS – Gifts made in a will.

BEST EVIDENCE – Primary evidence; the best evidence available. Evidence short of this is "secondary." That is, an original letter is "best evidence," and a photocopy is "secondary evidence."

BEYOND A REASONABLE DOUBT – The standard in a criminal case requiring that the jury be satisfied to a moral certainty that every element of a crime has been proven by the prosecution. This standard of proof does not require that the state establish absolute certainty by eliminating all doubt, but it does require that the evidence be so conclusive that all reasonable doubts are removed from the mind of the ordinary person.

BIAS – Inclination, bent, a pre-conceived opinion or a predisposition to decide a cause or an issue a certain way.

BOND – A certificate or evidence of a debt. Often used interchangeably with *bail.*

BRANDISHING A WEAPON – The act of showing a weapon to another person, typically the police or the victim.

BREACH – The breaking or violating of a law, right, obligation, or duty either by doing an act or failing to do an act.

BREAKING AND ENTERING – Breaking and entering a dwelling of another in nighttime with intent to commit a felony therein.

BREATHALYZER TEST – Test to determine content of alcohol in one arrested for operating a motor vehicle while under the influence of liquor by analyzing a breath sample.

BRIBE – A gift, not necessarily of monetary value, given to influence the conduct of the receiver.

BRIEF – A written statement prepared by the counsel arguing a case in court. It contains a summary of the facts of a case, the pertinent laws, and an argument of how the law applies to the facts supporting counsel's position.

BURDEN OF PROOF – The obligation of a party to establish by evidence a requisite degree of belief concerning a fact in the mind of the trier of fact or the court.

BURGLARY – The act of entering or remaining illegally in a movable or immovable structure, vehicle or dwelling with intent to commit a felony.

CALENDAR – List of cases scheduled for hearing in court.

CASE – A general term for an action, cause, suit, or controversy brought before the court for resolution.

CASE LAW – Law established by previous decisions of appellate courts, particularly the Supreme Court.

CASE NUMBER – See DOCKET NUMBER.

CAUSATION – The act which produces an effect.

CAUSE – A lawsuit, litigation, or action. Any question, civil or criminal, litigated or contested before a court of justice.

CAUSE OF ACTION – The facts that give rise to a lawsuit or a legal claim.

CERTIFICATION – 1. Written attestation. 2. Authorized declaration verifying that an instrument is a true and correct copy of the original.

CHALLENGE – An objection, such as when an attorney objects at a hearing to the seating of a particular person on a civil or criminal jury.

CHAMBERS – A judge's private office. A hearing in chambers takes place in the judge's office outside of the presence of the jury and the public.

CHANGE OF VENUE – Moving a lawsuit or criminal trial to another place for trial.

CHARGE – A formal allegation, as a preliminary step in prosecution, that a person has committed a specific offense, which is recorded in a complaint, information or indictment. To charge; To accuse. See INSTRUCTIONS.

CHARGING DOCUMENT – A written accusation alleging a defendant has committed an offense. Includes a citation, an indictment, information, and statement of charges.

CHIEF JUDGE – Presiding or Administrative Judge in a court.

CHILD ABUSE – Any form of cruelty to a child's physical, moral, or mental well-being.

CHILD MOLESTATION – Any form of indecent or sexual activity on, involving, or surrounding a child under the state's designated age.

CHILD SUPPORT – The legal obligation of parents to contribute to the economic maintenance, including education, of their children. Money paid by one parent to another toward the expenses of the children of the marriage.

CIRCUMSTANTIAL EVIDENCE – All evidence except eyewitness testimony. One example is physical evidence, such as fingerprints, from which an inference can be drawn.

CITATION – A reference to a source of legal authority. A direction to appear in court, as when a defendant is cited into court, rather than arrested.

CIVIL ACTION – Non-criminal case in which one private individual or business sues another to protect, enforce, or redress private or civil rights.

CIVIL CASE – A lawsuit brought to enforce, redress, or protect private rights or to gain payment for a wrong done to a person or party by another person or party. In general, all types of actions other than criminal proceedings.

CLAIM – The assertion of a right to money or property.

CLASS ACTION – A lawsuit brought by one or more persons on behalf of a larger group.

CLEAR AND CONVINCING EVIDENCE – Standard of proof commonly used in civil lawsuits and in regulatory agency cases. It governs the amount of proof that must be offered in order for the plaintiff to win the case.

CLERK – Officer of the court who files pleadings, motions, judgments, etc., issues process, and keeps records of court proceedings.

CLOSING ARGUMENT – The closing statement, by counsel, to the trier of facts after all parties have concluded their presentation of evidence.

CODE – A collection, compendium, or revision of laws, rules, and regulations enacted by legislative authority.

CODE OF PROFESSIONAL RESPONSIBILITY – The rules of conduct that govern the legal profession. The Code contains general ethical guidelines and specific rules written by the American Bar Association.

COLLATERAL – 1. Property that is pledged as security against a debt. 2. A person belonging to the same ancestral stock (a relation), but not in a direct line of descent.

COMMIT – 1. To execute, perpetrate, or carry out an act. To commit a crime. 2. To send a person to prison, asylum, or reformatory by a court order.

COMMITMENT – 1. The action of sending a person to a penal or mental institution. 2. The order directing an officer to take a person to a penal or mental institution.

COMMITMENT ORDER – A court order directing that an individual be kept in custody, usually in a penal or mental facility.

COMMUNITY PROPERTY – Property owned in common by husband and wife each having an undivided one-half interest by reason of their marital status. For example, the earnings of one spouse during the marriage do not belong solely to that spouse; the earnings are community property.

COMPARATIVE NEGLIGENCE – A legal doctrine by which acts of the opposing parties are compared to determine the liability of each party to the other, making each liable only for his or her percentage of fault. See also CONTRIBUTORY NEGLIGENCE.

COMPETENCY – Mental capacity of a person, especially with regard to his or her ability to stand trial and to assist counsel in his or her defense.

COMPLAINANT – The party who complains or sues; one who applies to the court for legal redress. Also called the *plaintiff*.

COMPLAINT – 1. The legal document that usually begins a civil lawsuit. It states the facts and identifies the action the court is asked to take. 2. Formal written charge that a person has committed a criminal offense.

COMPLY – To act in accordance with, to accept, to obey.

CONFESSION – Voluntary statement made by one who is a defendant in a criminal trial, which, if true, discloses his or her guilt.

CONFISCATE – To seize or take private property for public use (the police confiscated the weapon).

CONFLICT OF INTEREST – 1. A real or seeming incompatibility between one's private interests and one's public or fiduciary duties. 2. A real or seeming incompatibility between the interests of two of a lawyer's clients, such that the lawyer is disqualified from representing both clients if the dual representation adversely affects either client or if the clients do not consent.

CONSIDERATION – The cause, price, or impelling influence, which induces a party to enter into a contract.

CONSPIRACY – An agreement by two or more persons to commit an unlawful act; in criminal law, conspiracy is a separate offense from the crime that is the object of the conspiracy.

CONSTITUTIONAL RIGHT – A right guaranteed by the U. S. Constitution, interpreted by the federal courts; also, a right guaranteed by some other constitution (such as a state constitution).

CONTEMPT OF COURT – The finding of the court that an act was committed with the intent of embarrassing the court, disobeying its lawful orders, or obstructing the administration of justice in some way.

CONTINUANCE – The adjournment or postponement of a session, hearing, trial, or other proceeding until a future date.

CONTRACT – A legally enforceable agreement between two or more competent parties made either orally or in writing.

CONTRIBUTORY NEGLIGENCE – A legal doctrine that says if the plaintiff in a civil action for negligence also was negligent, he or she cannot recover damages from the defendant for the defendant's negligence. Most jurisdictions have abandoned the doctrine of contributory negligence in favor of *comparative negligence*.

CONTROLLED SUBSTANCE – Any of the drugs whose production and use are regulated by law, including narcotics, stimulants, and hallucinogens.

CONVICT – 1. A person who has been found guilty of a crime and is serving a sentence for that crime; a prison inmate. 2. To find a person guilty of an offense by either a trial or a plea of guilty.

CONVICTION – A judgment of guilty following a verdict or finding of guilty, a plea of guilty, or a plea of nolo contendere.

CORROBORATE – To support with evidence or authority; make more certain.

CORROBORATING EVIDENCE – Supplementary evidence that tends to strengthen or confirm the initial evidence.

CORROBORATION – Confirmation or support of a witness' statement or other fact.

COSTS – An allowance for expenses in prosecuting or defending a suit. Ordinarily this does not include attorney fees.

COUNSEL – A legal representative, attorney, lawyer.

COUNT – Each of the allegations of an offense listed in a charging document.

COUNTERCLAIM – A claim presented by a defendant in a civil lawsuit against the plaintiff. In essence, a counter lawsuit within a lawsuit.

COUNTERFEIT – To forge, to copy or imitate, without authority or right, and with the purpose to deceive or defraud, by passing off the copy as genuine.

COURT – 1. A unit of the judiciary authorized to decide disputed matters of fact, cases or controversies. 2. Figuratively, the judge or judicial officer. Judges sometimes use "court" to refer to themselves in the third person, as in "the court has read the briefs."

COURT ADMINISTRATOR/CLERK OF COURT – An officer appointed by the Court or elected to oversee the administrative, non-judicial activities of the court.

COURT COSTS – The expenses of prosecuting or defending a lawsuit, other than the attorneys' fees. An amount of money may be awarded to the successful party (and may be recoverable from the losing party) as reimbursement for court costs.

COURT ORDER – A written direction or command delivered by a court or judge.

COURT REPORTER – A person who makes a word-for-word record of what is said in court and produces a transcript of the proceedings upon request.

COURT, APPEALS – In some states, the highest appellate court, where it is the Court's discretion whether to hear the case on appeal.

COURT, DISTRICT – 1. Federal—A trial court with general Federal jurisdiction. 2. State—Meaning varies from state to state.

COURT, JUVENILE – A court having jurisdiction over cases involving children under a specified age, usually 18. Cases generally involve delinquent, dependent, and neglected children.

COURT, MUNICIPAL – A court having jurisdiction (usually civil and criminal) over cases arising within the city or community in which it sits.

COURT, SUPERIOR – Meaning varies from state to state.

COURT, TRAFFIC – A specialized court that hears crimes dealing with traffic offenses.

COURTROOM – The section of a courthouse in which the judge presides over the proceedings.

CREDIBILITY – The quality in a witness which makes his or her testimony believable.

CRIME – 1. An act of omission or commission in violation of law which carries criminal consequences. 2. Criminal activity in general relating to a specific time or place.

CRIMINAL – 1. One who has been convicted of a criminal offense. 2. That which is connected with the law of crimes; That which has the character of a crime (criminal justice; criminal intent).

CRIMINAL CASE – A case brought by the government against a person accused of committing a crime.

CRIMINAL INSANITY – Lack of mental capacity to do or abstain from doing a particular act; inability to distinguish right from wrong.

CRIMINAL RECORD – 1. Arrest record. A written account listing all the instances in which a person has been arrested. 2. A form completed by a police officer when a person is arrested.

CRIMINAL SUMMONS – An order commanding an accused to appear in court.

CROSS-CLAIM – A claim by codefendant or co-plaintiffs against each other and not against persons on the opposite side of the lawsuit.

CROSS-EXAMINATION – The questioning of a witness produced by the other side.

CUMULATIVE SENTENCES – Sentences for two or more crimes to run consecutively, rather than concurrently.

CUSTODY – 1. The care and control of a thing or person for inspection, preservation, or security. 2. The care, control, and maintenance of a child awarded by a court to one of the parents in a divorce or separation proceeding. 3. The detention of a person by virtue of lawful process or authority.

DAMAGES – Money awarded by a court to a person injured by the unlawful act or negligence of another person.

DECISION – The judgment reached or given by a court of law.

DECLARATORY JUDGMENT – A judgment of the court that explains what the existing law is or expresses the opinion of the court without the need for enforcement.

DECREE – An order of the court. A final decree is one that fully and finally disposes of the litigation. An *interlocutory* decree is a preliminary order that often disposes of only part of a lawsuit.

DEFAMATION – That which tends to injure a person's reputation. *Libel* is published defamation, whereas *slander* is spoken.

DEFAULT – A failure to respond to a lawsuit within the specified time.

DEFAULT-JUDGMENT – A judgment entered against a party who fails to appear in court, respond to the charges, or does not comply with an order, especially an order to provide or permit discovery.

DEFENDANT – 1. In a criminal case, the person accused of the crime. 2. In a civil case, the person being sued.

DEFENSE – 1. Defendant's statement of a reason why the plaintiff or prosecutor has no valid case against defendant, especially a defendant's answer, denial, or plea. 2. Defendant's method and strategy in opposing the plaintiff or the prosecution. 3. One or more defendants in a trial.

DEFENSE ATTORNEY – An attorney who represents the defendant.

DELIBERATION – The jury's decision-making process after hearing the evidence and closing arguments and being given the court's instructions.

DELINQUENCY, JUVENILE – Antisocial behavior by a minor; especially behavior that would be criminally punishable if the actor were an adult, but instead is usually punished by special laws pertaining only to minors.

DEPENDENT CHILD – A child who is homeless or without proper care through no fault of the parent, guardian, or custodian.

DEPORTATION – The act of removing a person to another country. Order issued by an immigration judge, expelling an alien from the United States. A deportation has certain consequences regarding the number of years within which a deportee may not legally immigrate. There are also criminal consequences for reentry within a prescribed time period.

DEPOSITION – A pretrial discovery device by which one party questions the other party or a witness for the other party. It usually takes place in the office of one of the lawyers, in the presence of a court reporter, who transcribes what is said. Questions are asked and answered orally as if in court, with opportunity given to the adversary to cross-examine. Occasionally, the questions are submitted in writing and answered orally.

DEPRIVATION OF CUSTODY – The court transfer of legal custody of a person from parents or legal guardian to another person, agency, or institution. It may be temporary or permanent.

DETENTION – The act or fact of holding a person in custody; confinement or compulsory delay.

DETENTION HEARING – In juvenile court, a judicial hearing, usually held after the filing of a petition, to determine interim custody of a minor pending a judgment.

DIRECT EVIDENCE – Proof of facts by witnesses who saw acts done or heard words spoken.

DIRECT EXAMINATION – The first questioning of witnesses by the party on whose behalf they are called.

DISBARMENT – Form of discipline of a lawyer resulting in the loss (often permanently) of that lawyer's right to practice law. It differs from censure (an official reprimand or condemnation) and from suspension (a temporary loss of the right to practice law).

DISCOVERY – The procedure by which one or both parties disclose evidence that will be used at trial. The specific tools of discovery include depositions, interrogatories and motions for the production of documents.

DISMISS – To terminate legal action involving outstanding charges against a defendant in a criminal case.

DISMISSAL WITH PREJUDICE – The dismissal of a case, by which the same cause of action cannot be brought against the defendant again at a later date.

DISMISSAL WITHOUT PREJUDICE – The dismissal of a case without preventing the plaintiff from bringing the same cause of action against the defendant in the future.

DISORDERLY CONDUCT – Any behavior, contrary to law, which disturbs the public peace or decorum, scandalizes the community, or shocks the public sense of morality.

DISPOSITION – A final settlement or determination. The court decision terminating proceedings in a case before judgment is reached, or the final judgment.

DISSENT – To disagree. An appellate court opinion setting forth the minority view and outlining the disagreement of one or more judges with the decision of the majority.

DISSOLUTION – The act of bringing to an end; termination. The dissolution of a marriage or other relationship.

DISTRICT ATTORNEY – A lawyer appointed or elected to represent the state in criminal cases in his or her respective judicial districts. See PROSECUTOR.

DIVERSION – 1. The process of removing some minor criminal traffic, or juvenile cases from the full judicial process, on the condition that the accused undergo some sort of rehabilitation or make restitution for damages. 2. Unauthorized use of funds.

DIVORCE – Legal dissolution of a marriage by a court. Also termed *dissolution* of marriage.

DOMESTIC VIOLENCE – An assault committed by one member of a household against another.

DRIVING WHILE INTOXICATED (DWI) – The unlawful operation of a motor vehicle while under the influence of drugs or alcohol. In some jurisdictions it is synonymous with DRIVING UNDER THE INFLUENCE (DUI), but in others, driving while intoxicated is a more serious offense than driving under the influence.

DRUNK DRIVING – The operation of a vehicle in an impaired state after consuming alcohol that when tested is above the state's legal alcohol limit.

DUE PROCESS OF LAW – The right of all persons to receive the guarantees and safeguards of the law and the judicial process. It includes such constitutional requirements as adequate notice, assistance of counsel, the right to remain silent, the right to a speedy and public trial, the right to an impartial jury, and the right to confront and secure witnesses.

ENTER A GUILTY PLEA – The formal statement before the court that the accused admits committing the criminal act.

EQUAL PROTECTION – The guarantee in the Fourteenth Amendment to the U.S. Constitution that all persons be treated equally by the law.

ESCROW – Money or a written instrument such as a deed that, by agreement between two parties, is held by a neutral third party (held in escrow) until all conditions of the agreement are met.

ESTATE – An estate consists of personal property (car, household items, and other tangible items), real property, and intangible property, such as stock certificates and bank accounts, owned in the individual name of a person at the time of the person's death. It does not include life insurance proceeds (unless the estate was made the beneficiary) or other assets that pass outside the estate (like joint tenancy assets).

EVICTION – Recovery of land or rental property from another by legal process.

EVIDENCE – Information presented in testimony or in documents that is used to persuade the fact finder (judge or jury) to decide the case for one side or the other.

EVIDENCE, CIRCUMSTANTIAL – Inferences drawn from proven facts.

EVIDENCE, DIRECT – Evidence in form of witness testimony, who actually saw, heard, or touched the subject of question.

EXAMINATION, DIRECT – The first examination of a witness by the counsel who called the witness to testify.

EXAMINATION, RECROSS – A second examination of a witness by the opposing counsel after the second examination (or redirect examination) by the counsel who called the witness to testify is completed.

EXAMINATION, REDIRECT – A second examination of a witness by the counsel who called the witness to testify. This examination is usually focused on certain matters that were discussed by the opposing counsel's examination.

EXCEPTIONS – Declarations by either side in a civil or criminal case reserving the right to appeal a judge's ruling upon a motion. Also, in regulatory cases, objections by either side to points made by the other side or to rulings by the agency or one of its hearing officers.

EXCLUSION OF WITNESSES – An order of the court requiring all witnesses to remain outside the courtroom until each is called to testify, except the plaintiff or defendant. The witnesses are ordered not to discuss their testimony with each other and may be held in contempt if they violate the order.

EXCULPATORY EVIDENCE – Evidence that tends to indicate that a defendant did not commit the alleged crime.

EXECUTE – To complete the legal requirements (such as signing before witnesses) that make a will valid. Also, to execute a judgment or decree means to put the final judgment of the court into effect.

EXHIBIT – A document or other item introduced as evidence during a trial or hearing.

EXPERT TESTIMONY – Testimony given in relation to some scientific, technical, or professional matter by experts, *i.e.*, person qualified to speak authoritatively by reason of their special training, skill, or familiarity with the subject.

EXPUNGEMENT – Official and formal erasure of a record or partial contents of a record.

EXTENUATING CIRCUMSTANCES – Circumstances that render a crime less aggravated, heinous, or reprehensible than it would otherwise be.

EYE WITNESS – One who saw the act, fact, or transaction to which he or she testifies.

FAILURE TO APPEAR – The act of not appearing in court after being presented with a subpoena or summons.

FAILURE TO COMPLY – The act of not following an order that is directed by the court.

FALSE ARREST – Any unlawful physical restraint of another's personal liberty, whether or not carried out by a peace officer.

FALSE IMPRISONMENT – The unlawful restraint by one person of another person's physical liberty.

FALSE PRETENSES – Representation of some fact or circumstance that is not true and is calculated to mislead, whereby a person obtains another's money or goods.

FELONY – A crime of a more serious nature than a misdemeanor, usually punishable by imprisonment in a penitentiary for more than a year and/or substantial fines.

FIDUCIARY – A person having a legal relationship of trust and confidence to another and having a duty to act primarily for the others benefit, *e.g.*, a guardian, trustee, or executor.

FILE – To place a paper in the official custody of the clerk of court to enter into the files or records of a case.

FIND GUILTY – For the judge or jury to determine and declare the guilt of the defendant.

FINDING – Formal conclusion by a judge or jury on issues of fact.

FINE – To sentence a person convicted of an offense to pay a penalty in money.

FINGERPRINT – The distinctive pattern of lines on human fingertips that are used as a method of identification in criminal cases.

FIREARM – A weapon that acts by force of gunpowder, such as a rifle, shotgun or revolver.

FORECLOSURE – Procedure by which mortgaged property is sold on default of the mortgagor in satisfaction of mortgage debt.

FORFEIT – To lose, or lose the right to.

FORGERY – The act of claiming one's own writing to be that of another.

FOSTER CARE – A program of parental care for children who do not have an in-home parental relationship with either biological or adoptive parents.

FRAUD – Intentional, unlawful deception to deprive another person of property or to injure that person in some other way.

GOOD CAUSE – Substantial reason, one that affords a legal excuse.

GOOD FAITH – An honest belief, the absence of malice, and the absence of design to defraud.

GROUNDS – A foundation or basis; points relied on.

GUILTY – Responsible for a delinquency, crime, or other offense; not innocent.

HANDCUFFS – Chains or shackles for the hands to secure prisoners.

HARASSMENT – Words, gestures, and actions that tend to annoy, alarm, and verbally abuse another person.

HEARING – A proceeding similar to a trial, without a jury, and usually of shorter duration.

HEARING, CONTESTED – A hearing held for the purpose of deciding issues or fact of law that both parties are disputing.

HEARSAY – Statements by a witness who did not see or hear the incident in question but heard about it from someone else. Hearsay is usually not admissible as evidence in court.

HIT AND RUN – Crime in which the driver of a vehicle leaves the scene of an accident without identifying himself or herself.

HOSTILE WITNESS – A witness whose testimony is not favorable to the party who calls him or her as a witness. A hostile witness may be asked leading questions and may be cross-examined by the party who calls him or her to the stand.

HUNG JURY – A jury whose members cannot agree upon a verdict.

HYPOTHETICAL QUESTION – An imaginary situation, incorporating facts previously admitted into evidence, upon which an expert witness is permitted to give an opinion as to a condition resulting from the situation.

ILLEGAL – Against, or not authorized by law; unlawful.

IMMUNITY – Grant by the court that assures someone will not face prosecution in return for providing evidence in a criminal proceeding.

IMPANEL – To seat a jury. When voir dire is finished and both sides have exercised their challenges, the jury is impaneled. The jurors are sworn in and the trial is ready to proceed.

IMPEACHMENT OF WITNESS – To call into question the truthfulness of a witness.

INADMISSIBLE – That which, under the rules of evidence, cannot be admitted as evidence in a trial or hearing.

INCAPACITY – The lack of power or the legal ability to act.

INCARCERATE – To confine in jail.

INCEST – Sexual intercourse between persons so closely related that marriage between them would be unlawful.

INCOMPETENCY – Lack of capacity to understand the nature and object of the proceedings, to consult with counsel, and to assist in preparing a defense.

INCRIMINATE – To make it appear that one is guilty of a crime.

INDICTMENT – A formal written accusation, issued by a grand jury, charging a party with a crime.

INDIGENT – Needy and poor. A defendant who can demonstrate his or her indigence to the court may be assigned a court-appointed attorney at public expense.

INFORMATION – A formal written document filed by the prosecutor detailing the criminal charges against the defendant. An alternative to an indictment, it serves to bring a defendant to trial.

INFRACTION – A violation of law, not punishable by imprisonment. Minor traffic offenses are generally considered infractions.

INJUNCTION – Writ or order by a court prohibiting a specific action from being carried out by a person or group.

INMATE – A person confined to a prison, penitentiary, or jail.

INNOCENT UNTIL PROVEN GUILTY – A belief in the American legal system which states that all people accused of a criminal act are considered not to have committed the crime until the evidence leaves no doubt in the mind of the court or the jury that the accused did or did not commit the crime.

INSTRUCTIONS – Judge's explanation to the jury before it begins deliberations of the questions it must answer and the applicable law governing the case. Also called *charge*.

INTENT – The purpose to use a particular means to bring about a certain result.

INTERROGATORIES – Written questions asked by one party in a lawsuit for which the opposing party must provide written answers.

INTERVENTION – An action by which a third person who may be affected by a lawsuit is permitted to become a party to the suit. Differs from the process of becoming an amicus curiae.

INVESTIGATION – A legal inquiry to discover and collect facts concerning a certain matter.

IRRELEVANT – Evidence not sufficiently related to the matter in issue.

ISSUE – 1. The disputed point in a disagreement between parties in a lawsuit. 2. To send out officially, as in to issue an order.

JAIL – A place of confinement that is more than a police station and less than a prison. It is usually used to hold persons convicted of misdemeanors or persons awaiting trial.

JOINT AND SEVERAL LIABILITY – A legal doctrine that makes each of the parties who are responsible for an injury liable for all the damages awarded in a lawsuit if the other parties responsible cannot pay.

JOYRIDING – The illegal taking of an automobile without intent to deprive the owner permanently of the vehicle, often involving reckless driving.

JUDGE – An elected or appointed public official with authority to hear and decide cases in a court of law.

JUDGMENT (JUDGMENT) – The final decision of the court, resolving the dispute; an opinion; an award.

JUDICIAL NOTICE – A court's recognition of the truth of basic facts without formal evidence.

JUDICIAL REVIEW – The authority of a court to review the official actions of other branches of government. Also, the authority to declare unconstitutional the actions of other branches.

JURISDICTION – 1. The legal authority of a court to hear and decide a case. 2. The geographic area over which the court has authority to decide cases.

JURISPRUDENCE – The study of law and the structure of the legal system.

JUROR – Member of the jury.

JUROR, ALTERNATE – Additional juror impaneled in case of sickness or disability of another juror.

JURY – A body of persons temporarily selected from the citizens of a particular district sworn to listen to the evidence in a trial and declare a verdict on matters of fact.

JURY BOX – The specific place in the courtroom where the jury sits during the trial.

JURY FOREMAN – The juror who chairs the jury during deliberations and speaks for the jury in court when announcing the verdict.

JURY TRIAL – Trial in which a jury decides issues of fact as opposed to trial only before a judge.

JURY, HUNG – A jury which is unable to agree on a verdict after a suitable period of deliberation.

JUSTICIABLE – Issues and claims capable of being properly examined in court.

JUVENILE – A young person who has not yet attained the age at which he or she should be treated as an adult for purposes of criminal law and other legal matters.

KIDNAPPING – The taking or detaining of a person against his or her will and without lawful authority.

KNOWINGLY – With knowledge, willfully or intentionally with respect to a material element of an offense.

LARCENY – Stealing or theft.

LAW – The combination of those rules and principles of conduct promulgated by legislative authority, derived from court decisions, and established by local custom.

LAW CLERKS – Persons trained in the law who assist judges in researching legal opinions.

LAWSUIT – An action between two or more persons in the courts of law, not a criminal matter.

LAY PERSON – One not trained in law.

LEADING QUESTION – One which instructs the witness how to answer or puts words in his mouth to be echoed back. One that suggests to the witness the answer desired.

LEASE – A contract by which owner of property grants to another the right to possess, use, and enjoy it for a specified period of time in exchange for payment of an agreed price (rent).

LEGAL AID – Professional legal services available usually to persons or organizations unable to afford such services.

LENIENCY – Recommendation for a sentence less than the maximum allowed.

LEWD CONDUCT – Behavior that is obscene, lustful, indecent, vulgar.

LIABILITY – Legal debts and obligations.

LIABLE – Legally responsible.

LIBEL – Published words or pictures that falsely and maliciously harm the reputation of a person. See DEFAMATION.

LIE DETECTOR – A machine which records by a needle on a graph varying emotional disturbances when answering questions truly or falsely, as indicated by fluctuations in blood pressure, respiration, or perspiration.

LIEN – A legal claim against another person's property as security for a debt. A lien does not convey ownership of the property, but gives the lien holder a right to have his or her debt satisfied out of the proceeds of the property if the debt is not otherwise paid.

LITIGANT – A party to a lawsuit. Litigation refers to a case, controversy, or lawsuit.

LITIGATION – A lawsuit.

MAGISTRATE – Judicial officer exercising some of the functions of a judge. It also refers in a general way to a judge.

MALFEASANCE – Evil doing, ill conduct; the commission of some act which is positively prohibited by law.

MALPRACTICE – Violation of a professional duty to act with reasonable care and in good faith without fraud or collusion. This term is usually applied to such conduct by doctors, lawyers, or accountants.

MANDATE – A judicial command or order proceeding from a court or judicial officer, directing the proper officer to enforce a judgment, sentence, or decree.

MASTER – An attorney who is appointed by the judges of a circuit court with the approval of the Chief Judge of the Court of Appeals, to conduct hearings and to make finding of facts, conclusions of law, and recommendations as to an appropriate order.

MATERIAL EVIDENCE – That quality of evidence which tends to influence the trier of fact because of its logical connection with the issue.

MATERIAL WITNESS – In criminal trial, a witness whose testimony is crucial to either the defense or prosecution.

MEDIATION – A form of *alternative dispute resolution* in which the parties bring their dispute to a neutral third party, who helps them agree on a settlement.

MEMORIALIZED – To mark by observation in writing.

MENTAL HEALTH – The wellness of a person's state of mind.

MERITS – Strict legal rights of the parties; a decision "on the merits" is one that reaches the right(s) of a party, as distinguished from disposition of a case on a ground not reaching the right(s) raised in an action; for example, entry of *nolle prosequi* before a criminal trial begins is a disposition other than on the merits, allowing trial on those charges at a later time without double jeopardy attaching; similarly, dismissal of a civil action on a preliminary motion raising a technicality, such as improper service of process, does not result in *res judicata* of an issue.

MISDEMEANOR – A lesser offense than a felony and generally punishable by fine or limited jail time, but not in a penitentiary.

MISTRIAL – An invalid trial caused by some legal error. When a judge declares a mistrial, the trial must start again from the beginning, including the selection of a new jury.

MITIGATING CIRCUMSTANCES – Those which do not constitute a justification or excuse for an offense but which may be considered as reasons for reducing the degree of blame.

MITIGATING FACTORS – Facts that do not constitute a justification or excuse for an offense but which may be considered as reasons for reducing the degree of blame.

MODIFICATION – A change, alteration, or amendment which introduces new elements into the details, or cancels some of them, but leaves the general purpose and effect of the subject matter intact.

MOOT – A moot case or a moot point is one not subject to a judicial determination because it involves an abstract question or a pretended controversy that has not yet actually arisen or has already passed. Mootness usually refers to a court's refusal to consider a case because the issue involved has been resolved prior to the court's decision, leaving nothing that would be affected by the court's decision.

MORAL TURPITUDE – Immorality. An element of crimes inherently bad, as opposed to crimes bad merely because they are forbidden by statute.

MOTION – Oral or written request made by a party to an action before, during, or after a trial asking the judge to issue a ruling or order in that party's favor.

MOTION DENIED – Ruling or order issued by the judge denying the party's request.

MOTION GRANTED – Ruling or order issued by the judge granting the party's request.

MUGSHOT – Pictures taken after a suspect is taken into custody (booked), usually used as an official photograph by police officers.

MURDER – The unlawful killing of a human being with deliberate intent to kill.

NEGLIGENCE – Failure to exercise the degree of care that a reasonable person would use under the same circumstances.

NEXT FRIEND – One acting without formal appointment as guardian for the benefit of an infant, a person of unsound mind not judicially declared incompetent, or other person under some disability.

NO-FAULT PROCEEDINGS – A civil case in which parties may resolve their dispute without a formal finding of error or fault.

NOT GUILTY – The form of verdict in criminal cases where the jury acquits the defendant, finds him or her not guilty.

NOT GUILTY BY REASON OF INSANITY – The jury or the judge must determine that the defendant, because of mental disease or defect, could not form the intent required to commit the offense.

NOTICE – Formal notification to the party that has been sued in a civil case of the fact that the lawsuit has been filed. Also, any form of notification of a legal proceeding.

NULL AND VOID – Having no force, legal power to bind, or validity.

OATH – Written or oral pledge by a witness to speak the truth.

OBJECT – To protest to the court against an act or omission by the opposing party.

OBJECTION – A protest to the court against an act or omission by the opposing party.

OBJECTION OVERRULED – A ruling by the court upholding the act or omission of the opposing party.

OBJECTION SUSTAINED – A ruling by the court in favor of the party making the objection.

OF COUNSEL – A phrase commonly applied to counsel employed to assist in the preparation or management of the case, or its presentation on appeal, but who is not the principal attorney for the party.

OFFENDER – One who commits a crime, such as a felony, misdemeanor, or other punishable unlawful act.

OFFENSE – A crime, such as a felony, misdemeanor, or other punishable unlawful act.

OFFER OF PROOF – Presentation of evidence to the court (out of the hearing of the jury) for the court's decision of whether the evidence is admissible.

ON A PERSON'S OWN RECOGNIZANCE – Release of a person from custody without the payment of any *bail* or posting of *bond*, upon the promise to return to court.

OPENING ARGUMENT – The initial statement made by attorneys for each side, outlining the facts each intends to establish during the trial.

OPENING STATEMENT – See OPENING ARGUMENT.

OPINION – A judge's written explanation of a decision of the court or of a majority of judges. A dissenting opinion disagrees with the majority opinion because of the reasoning and/or the principles of law on which the decision is based. A concurring opinion agrees with the decision of the court but offers further comment. A *per curiam opinion* is an unsigned opinion "of the court."

ORAL ARGUMENT – An opportunity for lawyers to summarize their position before the court and also to answer the judges' questions.

ORDER TO SHOW CAUSE – Court order requiring to appear and show cause why the court should not take a particular course of action. If the party fails to appear or to give sufficient reasons why the court should take no action, the court will take the action. In criminal cases, the defendant must show why probation should not be revoked.

ORDER, COURT – A written or verbal command from a court directing or forbidding an action.

ORDINANCE – An act of legislation of a local governing body such as a city, town or county.

OVERRULE – A judge's decision not to allow an objection. A decision by a higher court finding that a lower court decision was wrong.

OVERT ACT – An open act showing the intent to commit a crime.

PARALEGAL – A person with legal skills, but who is not an attorney, and who works under the supervision of a lawyer or who is otherwise authorized by law to use those legal skills.

PAROLE – Supervised release of a prisoner before the expiration of his or her sentence.

PAROLE EVIDENCE – Oral or verbal evidence rather than written. The Parole Evidence Rule limits the admissibility of parole evidence which would directly contradict the clear meaning of terms of a written contract.

PARTY – A person, business, or government agency actively involved in the prosecution or defense of a legal proceeding.

PATENT – A government grant giving an inventor the exclusive right to make or sell his or her invention for a term of years.

PATERNITY – Fatherhood.

PENALTY – Punishment, civil or criminal, generally referring to payment of money.

PENDING – Begun, but not yet completed. Thus, an action is pending from its inception until the rendition of its final judgment.

PEOPLE (PROSECUTION) – A state, for example, the People of the State of New York.

PEREMPTORY CHALLENGE – The right to challenge a juror without assigning a reason for the challenge.

PERJURY – A false statement given while under oath or in a sworn affidavit.

PERMANENT INJUNCTION – A court order requiring that some action be taken, or that some party refrain from taking action. It differs from forms of temporary relief, such as a *temporary restraining order* or *preliminary injunction.*

PERMANENT RESIDENT – One who lives in a location for a period of time and denotes it as their official address or residence.

PERSON IN NEED OF SUPERVISION – Juvenile found to have committed a status offense rather than a crime that would provide a basis for a finding of delinquency. Typical status offenses are habitual truancy, violating a curfew, or running away from home. These are not crimes, but they might be enough to place a child under supervision. In different states, status offenders might be called children in need of supervision or minors in need of supervision. See STATUS OFFENDERS.

PERSONAL PROPERTY – Tangible physical property (such as cars, clothing, furniture, and jewelry) and intangible personal property. This does not include real property such as land or rights in land.

PERSONAL RECOGNIZANCE – Pre-trial release based on the person's own promise that he or she will show up for trial (no bond required). Also referred to as *release on own recognizance* or ROR. See ON A PERSON'S OWN RECOGNIZANCE.

PETITION – A formal, written application to the court requesting judicial action on some matter.

PETITIONER – The person filing an action in a court of original jurisdiction. Also, the person who appeals the judgment of a lower court. The opposing party is called the *respondent.*

PETTY OFFENSE – An offense for which the authorized penalty does not exceed imprisonment for 3 months or a fine of $500.

PETTY THEFT – The act of taking and carrying away the personal property of another of a value usually below $100.00 with the intent to deprive the owner or possessor of it permanently.

PLAINTIFF – A person who initiates a lawsuit against another. Also called the *complainant.*

PLEA – In a criminal proceeding, it is the defendant's declaration in open court that he or she is guilty or not guilty. The defendant's answer to the charges made in the indictment or information.

PLEA BARGAIN – The process whereby the accused and the prosecutor in a criminal case work out a mutually satisfactory disposition of the case subject to court approval. Usually involves the defendant's pleading guilty to a lesser offense or to only one.

PLEADINGS – The written statements of fact and law filed by the parties to a lawsuit.

POLYGRAPH – Lie detector test and the apparatus for conducting the test.

POSSESSION OF DRUGS – The presence of drugs on the accused for recreational use or for the purpose to sell.

POST CONVICTION – A procedure by which a convicted defendant challenges the conviction and/or sentence on the basis of some alleged violation or error.

POSTPONEMENT – To put off or delay a court hearing.

POWER OF ATTORNEY – Formal authorization of a person to act in the interest of another person.

PRECEDENT – A previously decided case that guides the decision of future cases.

PRE-INJUNCTION – Court order requiring action or forbidding action until a decision can be made whether to issue a permanent injunction. It differs from a *temporary restraining order.*

PREJUDICE – A forejudgment, bias, a preconceived opinion.

PREJUDICIAL ERROR – Synonymous with *reversible error;* an error which warrants the appellate court in reversing the judgment before it.

PREJUDICIAL EVIDENCE – Evidence which might unfairly sway the judge or jury to one side or the other.

PRELIMINARY HEARING – Another term for *arraignment.*

PRELIMINARY INJUNCTION – In civil cases when it is necessary to preserve the status quo prior to trial, the court may issue a preliminary injunction or temporary restraining order ordering a party to carry out a specified activity.

PREPONDERANCE OF THE EVIDENCE – Evidence which is of greater weight or more convincing than the evidence which is offered in opposition to it.

PRE-SENTENCE REPORT – A report to the sentencing judge containing background information about the crime and the defendant to assist the judge in making his or her sentencing decision.

PRESUMPTION – An inference of the truth or falsity of a proposition or fact, that stands until rebutted by evidence to the contrary.

PRESUMPTION OF INNOCENCE – A hallowed principle of criminal law that a person is innocent of a crime until proven guilty. The government has the burden of proving every element of a crime beyond a reasonable doubt and the defendant has no burden to prove his innocence.

PRESUMPTION OF LAW – A rule of law that courts and judges shall draw a particular inference from a particular fact, or from particular evidence.

PRE-TRIAL CONFERENCE – A meeting between the judge and the lawyers involved in a lawsuit to narrow the issues in the suit, agree on what will be presented at the trial, and make a final effort to settle the case without a trial.

PRISON – A federal or state public building or other place for the confinement of persons. It is used as either a punishment imposed by the law or otherwise in the course of the administration of justice. Also known as penitentiary, penal institution, adult correctional institution, or jail.

PRIVILEGE – A legal right, exemption or immunity granted to a person, company or class, that is beyond the common advantages of other citizens.

PRIVILEGED COMMUNICATIONS – Confidential communications to certain persons that are protected by law against any disclosure, including forced disclosure in legal proceedings. Communications between lawyer and client, physician and patient, psychotherapist and patient, priest, minister, or rabbi and penitent are typically privileged.

PROBABLE CAUSE – A reasonable belief that a crime has or is being committed; the basis for all lawful searches, seizures, and arrests.

PROBATION – A sentence imposed for the commission of a crime whereby a convicted criminal offender is released into the community, usually under conditions and under the supervision of a probation officer, instead of incarceration. A violation of probation can lead to its revocation and to imprisonment.

PROBATION BEFORE JUDGMENT (PBJ) – A conditional avoidance of imposition of sentence after conviction; failure to satisfy the conditions may cause imposition of sentence after a finding of violation of probation.

PROCEDURAL LAW – The method, established normally by rules to be followed in a case; the formal steps in a judicial proceeding.

PROFFER – An offer of proof as to what the evidence would be if a witness were called to testify or answer a question.

PROOF – Any fact or evidence that leads to a judgment of the court.

PROSECUTING ATTORNEY – See PROSECUTOR and DISTRICT ATTORNEY.

PROSECUTION – A proceeding instituted and carried on in order to determine the guilt or innocence of the accused.

PROSECUTOR – A trial lawyer representing the government in a criminal case and the interests of the state in civil matters. In criminal cases, the prosecutor has the responsibility of deciding who and when to prosecute.

PROSTITUTION – The performance or agreement to perform a sexual act for hire.

PROTECTIVE ORDER – A court order to protect a person from further harassment, service of process, or discovery.

PROXIMATE CAUSE – The act that caused an event to occur. A person generally is liable only if an injury was proximately caused by his or her action or by his or her failure to act when he or she had a duty to act.

PUBLIC DEFENDER – An attorney appointed by a court or employed by a government agency whose work consists primarily of defending people who are unable to hire a lawyer due to economic reasons.

PUNITIVE DAMAGES – Money awarded to an injured person, over and above the measurable value of the injury, in order to punish the person who hurt him.

PURGE – To clean or clear, such as eliminating inactive records from court files; with respect to civil contempt, to cure the noncompliance that caused the contempt finding.

QUASH – To overthrow, to vacate, to annul or make void.

QUASI JUDICIAL – Authority or discretion vested in an officer whose acts partake of a judicial character.

RAP SHEET – A listing of all the criminal convictions against an individual.

RAPE – Unlawful intercourse with an individual without their consent.

RAPE, STATUTORY – See STATUTORY RAPE.

REASONABLE DOUBT, BEYOND A – The degree of certainty required for a juror to legally find a criminal defendant guilty. An accused person is entitled to acquittal if, in the minds of the jury, his or her guilt has not been proved beyond a "reasonable doubt"; that state of mind of jurors in which they cannot say they feel a persisting conviction as to the truth of the charge.

REASONABLE PERSON – A phrase used to denote a hypothetical person who exercises qualities of attention, knowledge, intelligence, and judgment that society requires of its members for the protection of his or her own interest and the interests of others. Thus, the test of negligence is based on either a failure to do something that a reasonable person, guided by considerations that ordinarily regulate conduct, would do, or on the doing of something that a reasonable and prudent (wise) person would not do.

REBUTTAL – Evidence given to explain, counteract, or disprove facts given by the opposing counsel.

RECKLESS DRIVING – Operation of a motor vehicle that shows a reckless disregard of possible consequences and indifference of other's rights.

RECOGNIZANCE – The practice which enables an accused awaiting trial to be released without posting any security other than a promise to appear before the court at the proper time. Failure to appear in court at the proper time is a separate crime.

RECORD – All the documents and evidence plus transcripts of oral proceedings in a case.

RECUSE – The process by which a judge is disqualified from hearing a case, on his or her own motion or upon the objection of either party.

RE-DIRECT EXAMINATION – Opportunity to present rebuttal evidence after one's evidence has been subjected to cross-examination.

REDRESS – To set right; to remedy; to compensate; to remove the causes of a grievance.

REGULATION – A rule or order prescribed for management or government.

REHEARING – Another hearing of a civil or criminal case by the same court in which the case was originally heard.

RELEVANT – Evidence that helps to prove a point or issue in a case.

REMAND – The act of sending a case back to the trial court and ordering the trial court to conduct limited new hearings or an entirely new trial.

REMEDY – The means by which a right is enforced or the violation of a right is prevented, redressed or compensated.

REPLY – The response by a party to charges raised in a pleading by the other party.

REPORT – An official or formal statement of facts or proceedings.

RESPONDENT – The party who makes an answer to a bill or other proceedings in equity; also refers to the party against whom an appeal is brought. Sometimes called an *appellee*.

REST – A party is said to *rest* or *rest* its case when it has presented all the evidence it intends to offer.

RESTITUTION – Act of giving the equivalent for any loss, damage or injury.

RESTRAINING ORDER – A court order forbidding the defendant from doing any action or threatened action until a hearing on the application can be conducted.

RETAINER – Act of the client in employing the attorney or counsel. Also denotes the fee the client pays when he or she retains the attorney to act for him or her.

RETURN – A report to a judge by police on the implementation of an arrest or search warrant. Also, a report to a judge in reply to a subpoena, civil or criminal.

REVERSE – An action of a higher court in setting aside or revoking a lower court decision.

REVERSIBLE ERROR – A procedural error during a trial or hearing sufficiently harmful to justify reversing the judgment of a lower court. See PREJUDICIAL ERROR.

REVOKE – To annul or make void by recalling or taking back.

RIGHTS, CONSTITUTIONAL – The rights of a person guaranteed by the state or federal constitutions.

ROBBERY – The act of taking money, personal property, or any other article of value that is in the possession of another done by means of force or fear.

RULE – An established standard, guide, or regulation.

RULE OF COURT – An order made by a court having competent jurisdiction. Rules of court are either general or special; the former are the regulations by which the practice of the court is governed, the latter are special orders made in particular cases.

RULES OF EVIDENCE – Standards governing whether evidence in a civil or criminal case is admissible.

SANCTION – A punitive act designed to secure enforcement by imposing a penalty for its violation. For example, a sanction may be imposed for failure to comply with discovery orders.

SEALING – The closure of court records to inspection, except to the parties.

SEARCH AND SEIZURE – A practice whereby a person or place is searched and evidence useful in the investigation and prosecution of a crime is seized or taken. The search is conducted after an order is issued by a judge.

SEARCH WARRANT – An order issued by a judge or magistrate commanding a sheriff, constable, or other officer to search a specified location.

SELF-DEFENSE – Claim that an act otherwise criminal was legally justifiable because it was necessary to protect a person or property from the threat or action of another.

SELF-INCRIMINATION – Acts or declarations by which one implicates oneself in a crime.

SENTENCE – The judgment formally pronounced by the court or judge upon the defendant after his or her conviction by imposing a punishment to be inflicted either in the form of a fine, incarceration or probation.

SENTENCE REPORT – A document containing background material on a convicted person. It is prepared to guide the judge in the imposition of a sentence. Sometimes called a *pre-sentence report*.

SEPARATE MAINTENANCE – Allowance ordered to be paid by one spouse to the other for support while the spouses are living apart but not divorced.

SEPARATION – An arrangement whereby a husband and wife live apart from each other while remaining married either by mutual consent or by a judicial order.

SERVICE – The delivery of a legal document, such as a complaint, summons, or subpoena, notifying a person of a lawsuit or other legal action taken against him or her. Service, which constitutes formal legal notice, must be made by an officially authorized person in accordance with the formal requirements of the applicable laws.

SERVICE OF PROCESS – Notifying a person that he or she has been named as a party to a lawsuit or has been accused of some offense. Process consists of a summons, citation or warrant, to which a copy of the complaint is attached.

SETTLEMENT – An agreement between parties that dictates what is being received from one party to the other.

SEXUAL MOLESTATION – Illegal sex acts performed against a minor by a parent, guardian, relative or acquaintance.

SHERIFF – Elected officer of a county whose job is to conserve peace within his or her territorial jurisdiction as well as aid in the criminal and civil court processes.

SHOPLIFTING – The willful taking and concealing of merchandise from a store or business establishment with the intention of using the goods for one's personal use without paying the purchase price.

SHOW CAUSE – An order requiring a person to appear in court and present reasons why a certain order, judgment, or decree should not be issued.

SIDEBAR – A conference between the judge and lawyers, usually in the courtroom, out of earshot of the jury and spectators.

SLANDER – False and defamatory spoken words tending to harm another's reputation, community standing, office, trade, business, or means of livelihood. See DEFAMATION.

SMALL CLAIMS COURT – A court that handles civil claims for small amounts of money. People often represent themselves rather than hire an attorney.

SODOMY – Oral or anal copulation between humans, or between humans or animals.

SOVEREIGN IMMUNITY – The doctrine that the government, state or federal, is immune to lawsuit unless it gives its consent.

SPEEDY TRIAL – The right of an accused to a speedy trial as guaranteed by the 6th Amendment of the United States Constitution.

STANDARD OF PROOF – There are essentially three standards of proof applicable in most court proceedings. In criminal cases, the offense must be proven *beyond a reasonable doubt,* the highest standard. In civil cases and neglect and dependency proceedings, the lowest standard applies by a mere *preponderance of the evidence,* (more likely than not). In some civil cases, and in juvenile proceedings such as a permanent termination of parental rights, an provide linguistic mediation standard applies, proof by *clear and convincing evidence.*

STANDING – The legal right to bring a lawsuit. Only a person with something at stake has standing to bring a lawsuit.

STATEMENT, CLOSING – The final statements by the attorneys to the jury or court summarizing the evidence that they have established and the evidence that the other side has failed to establish. Also known as *closing argument.*

STATEMENT, OPENING – Outline or summary of the nature of the case and of the anticipated proof presented by the attorney to the jury before any evidence is submitted. Also known as *opening argument.*

STATUTE – A formal, written statement by legislature declaring, commanding, or prohibiting something.

STATUTE OF LIMITATIONS – The time within a plaintiff must begin a lawsuit (in civil cases) or a prosecutor must bring charges (in criminal cases). There are different statutes of limitations at both the federal and state levels for different kinds of lawsuits or crimes.

STATUTORY RAPE – The unlawful sexual intercourse with a person under an age set by statute, regardless of whether they consent to the act.

STAY – The act of stopping a judicial proceeding by order of the court.

STIPULATE – An agreement by attorneys on both sides of a civil or criminal case about some aspect of the case; *e.g.,* to extend the time to answer, to adjourn the trial date, or to admit certain facts at the trial.

SUBMIT – To yield to the will of another.

SUBPOENA – An order of the court which requires a person to be present at a certain time and place to give testimony upon a certain matter. Failure to appear may be punishable as a contempt of court.

SUE – To commence legal proceedings for recovery of a right.

SUIT – Any proceeding by one person or persons against another in a court of law.

SUMMARY JUDGMENT – A decision made on the basis of statements and evidence presented for the record without a trial. It is used when there is no dispute as to the facts of the case, and one party is entitled to judgment as a matter of law.

SUMMONS – A notice to a defendant that he or she has been sued or charged with a crime and is required to appear in court. A jury *summons* requires the person receiving it to report for possible jury duty.

SUPPRESS – To forbid the use of evidence at a trial because it is improper or was improperly obtained. See also EXCLUSIONARY RULE.

SUPPRESSION HEARING – A hearing on a criminal defendant's motion to prohibit the prosecutor's use of evidence alleged to have been obtained in violation of the defendant's rights. This hearing is held outside of the presence of the jury, either prior to or at trial. The judge must rule as a matter of law on the motion.

SUSTAIN – To maintain, to affirm, to approve.

SWEAR – To put to oath and declare as truth.

TEMPORARY RELIEF – Any form of action by a court granting one of the parties an order to protect its interest pending further action by the court.

TEMPORARY RESTRAINING ORDER – A judge's order forbidding certain actions until a full hearing can be held. Usually of short duration. Often referred to as a *TRO.*

TENANCY – An interest in realty which passes to the tenant.

TESTIFY – To make a declaration under oath in a judicial inquiry for the purpose of establishing or proving some fact.

TESTIMONY – The evidence given by a witness under oath. It does not include evidence from documents and other physical evidence.

THEFT – The act of stealing or the taking of property without the owner's consent.

THIRD-PARTY – A person, business, or government agency not actively involved in a legal proceeding, agreement, or transaction.

THIRD-PARTY CLAIM – An action by the defendant that brings a third party into a lawsuit.

TITLE – Legal ownership of property, usually real property or automobiles.

TORT – A civil injury or wrong committed on the person or property of another. A tort is an infringement on the rights of an individual, but not founded on a contract. The most common tort action is a suit for damages sustained in an automobile accident. See EX DELICTO.

TRANSCRIPT – A written, word-for-word record of what was said, either in a proceeding such as a trial or during some other conversation, as in a transcript of a hearing or oral deposition.

TRANSITORY – Actions are "transitory" when they might have taken place anywhere, and are "local" when they could occur only in some particular place.

TRESPASSING – Unlawful interference with one's person, property and rights.

TRIAL – A judicial examination and determination of issues between parties before a court that has jurisdiction.

TRIAL COURT – See TRIAL, COURT (BENCH).

TRIAL, COURT (BENCH) – A trial where the jury is waived and the case is seen before the judge alone.

TRIAL, SPEEDY – The Sixth Amendment of the Constitution guarantees the accused to an immediate trial in accordance with prevailing rules, regulations and proceedings of law.

TRO – See TEMPORARY RESTRAINING ORDER.

UNCONSCIONABILITY – An absence of meaningful choice on the part of one of the parties to a contract, and contract terms which are unreasonably favorable to the other party.

UNCONSTITUTIONAL – That which is contrary to or in conflict with the federal or state constitutions.

UNDUE INFLUENCE – Whatever destroys free will and causes a person to do something he would not do if left to himself.

UNEMPLOYMENT – State or condition of not being employed.

UNILATERAL – One-sided, ex parte, or having a relation to only one of two or more persons or things.

UNSECURED – In bankruptcy proceedings, for the purposes of filing a claim, a claim is unsecured if there is no collateral, or to the extent the value of collateral is less than the amount of the debt.

VACATE – To render an act void; to set aside.

VENUE – The proper geographical area (county, city, or district) in which a court with jurisdiction over the subject matter may hear a case.

VERDICT – The opinion of a jury, or a judge where there is no jury, on the factual issues of a case.

VICTIM – A person who is the object of a crime or civil wrongdoing.

VICTIM IMPACT STATEMENT – A statement during sentencing which informs the sentencer of the impact of the crime on the victim or the victim's family.

VIOLATION – The act of breaking, infringing, or transgressing the law.

VISITATION – The right given to a non-custodial parent to see his or her child at court appointed times.

WAIVE (RIGHTS) – A knowing and knowledgeable act to abandon, renounce or surrender a person's rights.

WAIVER OF IMMUNITY – A means authorized by statute by which a witness, before testifying or producing evidence, may relinquish the right to refuse to testify against himself or herself, thereby making it possible for his or her testimony to be used against him or her in future proceedings.

WAIVER OF RIGHTS – See WAIVE (RIGHTS).

WARRANT – Most commonly, a court order authorizing law enforcement officers to make an arrest or conduct a search. An affidavit seeking a warrant must establish probable cause by detailing the facts upon which the request is based.

WARRANT OF ARREST – See WARRANT, ARREST.

WARRANT, ARREST – An order of a court directing the sheriff or other officer to seize a particular person to answer a complaint of otherwise appear before the court.

WARRANT, SEARCH – A written order directing a law-enforcement officer to conduct a search of a specified place and to seize any evidence directly related to the criminal offense.

WEAPON – An instrument used or designed to be used to threaten, injure or kill someone.

WEIGHT OF THE EVIDENCE – The persuasiveness of certain evidence when compared with other evidence that is presented.

WILL – A legal declaration that disposes of a person's property when that person dies. See TESTAMENT.

WILLFUL – A "willful" act is one done intentionally, as distinguished from an act done carelessly or inadvertently.

WITH PREJUDICE – Applied to orders of judgment dismissing a case, meaning that the plaintiff is forever barred from bringing a lawsuit on the same claim or cause.

WITHOUT PREJUDICE – A claim or cause dismissed without prejudice may be the subject of a new lawsuit.

WITNESS – 1. One who testifies to what they have seen, heard or otherwise observed. 2. (v) To subscribe one's name to a document for the purpose of authenticity.

WITNESS STAND – The space in the courtroom occupied by a witness while testifying.

WITNESS, DEFENSE – A non-hostile witness that is called by the defense counsel to assist in proving the defense's case.

WITNESS, EXPERT – A witness who is qualified by knowledge, skill, experience, training or education to provide a scientific, technical or specialized opinion of the subject about which he or she is to testify. That knowledge must generally be such as is not normally possessed by the average person.

WITNESS, HOSTILE – A witness whose relationship to the opposing party is such that his or her testimony may be prejudiced against that party. A witness declared to be hostile may be asked leading questions and is subject to cross-examination by the party that called him or her.

WITNESS, MATERIAL – A witness who can give testimony relating to a particular matter that very few others, if any, can give.

WITNESS, PROSECUTION – The person whose complaint commences a criminal prosecution and whose testimony is mainly relied on to secure a conviction at the trial.

WRIT – A court's written order commanding the addressee to do or refrain from doing some specified act.

ZONING – The division of a city by legislative regulation into districts, and the design of regulations having to do with structural and architectural design and use of buildings.

Latin Terms

ACTION IN REM – Proceeding "against the thing" as compared to personal actions (*in personam*). Usually a proceeding where property is involved.

AD LITEM – A Latin term meaning for the purposes of the lawsuit. For example, a *guardian ad litem* is a person appointed by the court to protect the interests of a minor or legally incompetent person in a lawsuit.

AMICUS CURIAE (A-MI'KUS KU'RIE) – A friend of the court. One not a party to a case who volunteers to offer information on a point of law or some other aspect of the case to assist the court in deciding a matter before it.

CAVEAT – A warning; a note of caution.

CAVEAT EMPTOR – "Let the buyer beware." Encourages a purchaser to examine, judge, and test for himself.

CERTIORI – A means of getting an appellate court to review a lower court's decision. The loser of a case will often ask the appellate court to issue a writ of certiorari, which orders the lower court to convey the record of the case to the appellate court and to certify it as accurate and complete. If an appellate court grants a writ of certiorari, it agrees to take the appeal. This is often referred to as granting cert.

DE NOVO – A new. A *trial de novo* is a new trial of a case.

ET AL – And others.

ET SEQ – An abbreviation for et sequentes, or et sequentia, "and the following," ordinarily used in referring to a section of statutes.

EX PARTE – On behalf of only one party, without notice to any other party. For example, a request for a search warrant is an ex parte proceeding, since the person subject to the search is not notified of the proceeding and is not present at the hearing.

EX PARTE PROCEEDING – The legal procedure in which only one side is represented. It differs from *adversary system* or adversary proceeding.

EX POST FACTO – After the fact. The Constitution prohibits the enactment of ex post facto laws. These are laws that permit conviction and punishment for a lawful act performed before the law was changed and the act made illegal.

GUARDIAN AD LITEM – A person appointed by a court to look after the interests of an infant, child, or incompetent during court proceedings.

HABEAS CORPUS – A writ which commands that a party be brought before a court or judge and to protect him or her from unlawful imprisonment or custody.

HEARING DE NOVO – A full new hearing.

IN CAMERA – In chambers, or in private. A hearing in camera takes place in the judge's office outside of the presence of the jury and the public.

IN FORMA PAUPERIS – "In the manner of a pauper." Permission given to a person to sue without payment of court fees on claim of indigence or poverty.

IN LOCO PARENTIS – "In the place of the parent," refers to actions of a custodian, guardian, or other person acting in the parent's place.

IN REM – A procedural term used to designate proceedings or actions instituted against the thing in contrast to actions instituted *in personam* or against the person.

LIMINE – A motion requesting that the court not allow certain evidence that might prejudice the jury.

MANDAMUS – A writ issued by a court ordering a public official to perform an act.

MENS REA – The "guilty mind" necessary to establish criminal responsibility.

MOTION IN LIMINE – A written motion which is usually made before or after the beginning of a jury trial for a protective order against prejudicial questions and statements.

NOLLE PROSEQUI – Decision by a prosecutor not to go forward with charging a crime. It translates, "I do not choose to prosecute." Also loosely called nolle pros.

NOLO CONTENDRE – A plea of no contest. In many jurisdictions, it is an expression that the matter will not be contested, but without an admission of guilt. In other jurisdictions, it is an admission of the charges and is equivalent to a guilty plea.

NON COMPOS MENTIS – Not of sound mind; insane.

NON OBSTANTE VERDICTO (N.O.V.) – Notwithstanding the verdict. A verdict entered by the judge contrary to a jury's verdict.

NUNC PRO TUNC – A legal phrase applied to acts which
are allowed after the time when they should be done, with a
retroactive effect.

PER CURIUM OPINION – An unsigned *opinion* of the court.

PRIMA FACIE CASE – A case that is sufficient and has the
minimum amount of evidence necessary to allow it to continue
in the judicial process.

PRO BONO PUBLICO – For the public good. Lawyers representing clients without a fee are said to be working pro bono publico.

PRO SE – A Latin term meaning "on one's own behalf"; in
courts, it refers to persons who present their own cases without
lawyers. See IN PROPIA PERSONA and PRO PER.

QUID PRO QUO – What for what; something for something;
giving one valuable thing for another.

RES JUDICATA – A rule of civil law that once a matter has
been litigated and final judgment has been rendered by the trial
court, the matter cannot be relitigated by the parties in the same
court, or any other trial court.

RESPONDEAT SUPERIOR – "Let the master answer." The
doctrine which holds that employers are responsible for the acts
and omissions of their employees and agents, when done within
the scope of the employees' duties.

SUA SPONTE – A Latin phrase which means on one's own
behalf. Voluntary, without prompting or suggestion.

SUBPOENA DUCES TECUM – A court order commanding a
witness to bring certain documents or records to court.

TRIAL DE NOVO – A new tri or retrial held in an appellate
court in which the whole case is heard as if no trial had been
heard in the lower court or administrative agency.

VOIR DIRE – "To speak the truth": the preliminary examination
which the court and attorneys make of prospective jurors to
determine their qualification and suitability to serve as juror.